南京利济巷慰安所旧址 | 陈列馆展陈艺术图集 | *NANJING MUSEUM OF SITE OF LIJIXIANG COMFORT STATIONS ART ATLAS EXHIBIT* |

泪滴塑空间

南京 利济巷慰安所旧址 陈列馆展陈艺术图集

东南大学出版社

TEARS SCULPTURE SPACE

NANJING MUSEUM
OF SITE OF LIJIXIANG COMFORT STATIONS
ART ATLAS EXHIBIT

主编：朱成山、任　睿
摄影：任　睿
文字说明：陶晓杰
装帧设计：李　涛

Chief Editor:Zhu Chengshan, Ren Rui
Photographer:Ren Rui
Describer:Tao Xiaojie
Design:Li Tao

序

泪滴立馆　承载记忆

2015年12月1日，亚洲乃至世界上目前保存最为完整、面积最大的侵华日军慰安所建筑群——南京利济巷慰安所旧址陈列馆正式建成开放了。中宣部副部长、国务院新闻办副主任崔玉英，江苏省委常委、宣传部长王燕文，南京市委常委、宣传部长徐宁等领导出席了开幕式，新华社、中新社、新华日报、扬子晚报、南京日报等众多媒体作了大篇幅的报道，开馆的消息像长了翅膀一样，迅速传遍了五湖四海。我作为这项工程建设的策划者、参与者、管理者和负责者，筹建工程过往的一幕幕，仿佛如昨，不断地浮现在眼前。

一波三折，承担筹建"主角"

世上的人和事，原本是有一定缘分的。不管你信还是不信，有些事只要与你有缘，沾上了，推都推不掉。我与南京利济巷慰安所旧址陈列馆建设工程，就是具有代表性的一例。

记得利济巷旧址还是在白下区管辖的时候，时任区长的曹永宁曾经找到我，说是利济巷所在地位于南京规划中的重点历史文化街区长白街，与科巷菜场相交的8幢二层砖混结构民国建筑，2008年被拆迁后一直空置，并且垃圾成堆，房屋破损严重，影响市容观瞻，白下区政府准备修复，建设成为慰安所旧址陈列馆。后来在区划调整中，该地块划入秦淮区管辖，该区常务副区长薛凤冠找到我，说秦淮区计划修建慰安所陈列馆，请我作历史顾问，我愉快地答应。再后来，南京市的领导一度要求市文广新局负责筹建，其副局长颜一平请我支持，我岂有不从之理。没有想到的是，一波三折之后，南京市领导最终将这项工程复建的任务直接交给我，并且明确指示建成后，要成为侵华日军南京大屠杀遇难同胞纪念馆（以下简称"纪念馆"）的一座分馆来运行。说实话，作为馆长，当时我曾经以正在建设纪念馆扩容工程，新建以"胜利"为主题陈列馆，同时申报南京大屠杀世界记忆遗产和筹办首次国家公祭等工作任务繁重为由，委婉表达了推辞之意。但南京市委和市政府的主要领导，既批评又鼓励我说，大家都忙，忙是好事，你牵头负责，同时可以委托代建。

面对组织和领导的信任，2014年10月，我在任务超负荷的情况下，接下了复建利济巷慰安所旧址工程的重任。

以旧修旧，锻造精品工程

可能与我从军 20 年的经历有关联，凡是接下了任务，我就会全心全意并且想方设法出色地完成。

在接受利济巷工程后，我主要做了五件事：

一是首先去了南京大学建筑设计院（以下简称"设计院"），找到赵辰教授和冷天老师，委托他们尽快拿出利济巷修复工程的建筑设计方案。其实，我在参与白下区和秦淮区的多轮有关利济巷修复工程的研讨会上，听到过并研讨过他们的方案，当时我只是配角和旁观者，但对于他们的设计理念和基本定位有所了解，容易上手，事半功倍。果然，当我与侯曙光副馆长向他们说明意图后，一拍即合，不仅其方案很快得到市领导的充分肯定和有关职能部门的批准，而且在修复工程期间，双方抱着对工程负责的态度，密切配合，反复修改，集思广益，精益求精，作为学术研究与探讨的实践项目，成为强强联合、充分信任与合作的好伙伴。需要特别强调的是，对纪念性场馆特别是旧址陈列馆来说，建筑艺术与陈列艺术是相辅相成、相得益彰的。换句话说，没有好的有特色的建筑艺术设计，展陈艺术就没有立足之基和充分拓展的空间。

二是迅速组织了撰写展陈大纲的团队，挑选了一批年轻学者，要求他们尽快拿出一个好的展陈脚本。考虑到同时要承担纪念馆以"胜利"为主题的新展厅实际状况，还出于对纪念馆新的研究人员的锻炼和培养，我特意有选择地组织了 4 位年轻人，即研究保管处副处长袁志秀、研究科副科长曹林、研究科两位硕士研究生张国松、刘广建，还抽调保管科副科长孙红亮和硕士研究生秦逸等人负责相关文物挑选，由我亲自牵头负责和修改统稿。经过一番讨论，确定了用 6 个展览组成完整的展陈架构，即一个基本陈列、一个原址陈列、4 个专题陈列。将 A 区小楼辟为基本陈列展厅，定名为"二战"中的性奴隶——日军"慰安妇"制度及其罪行展；将 B 区小楼辟为原址陈列，定名为金陵梦魇——南京日军慰安所与"慰安妇"史实展；将 C 区 4 幢小楼辟为专题陈列展厅，分别定名为沪城性奴泪——上海慰安所与日军"慰安妇"制度罪证展、遍布中国的日军慰安所——中国"慰安妇"血泪记忆展、伤痛记忆与控诉——来自朝鲜半岛的日军"慰安妇"受害史实展、众多国籍的性奴隶——太平洋战争与日军"慰安妇"制度罪行展。结构确定后，进行分工负责，几名年轻的学者分头找资料，具体寻找和撰写所承担的展陈文字、图片和文物，然后交我修改把关，再发回补充修订，反反复复的几个回合下来，大纲趋向成熟，再请来上海师范大学的苏智良教授、南京师范大学的经盛鸿教授、南大设计院的赵辰教授、城建集团的陈永战总工程师等专家，有针对性地提出修改意见，最后报请有关部门和领导审批，终于形成了一份有特色并像模像样的展陈大纲。

三是奉命挑选代建施工单位，找到了南京市城建集团项目工程公司（以下简称"项目公司"），委托他们来利济巷组织工程建设。由于利济巷修复项目被定为保密工程，可以委托施工单位。为什么要委托"项目公司"，理由很简单，他们曾参与南京站、南京南站、模范马路、龙蟠路等大项目的建设，是南京市属的一支能打硬仗、大仗，攻难克艰和善于合作的建筑公司，还因为他们曾经出色地完成了纪念馆二期扩建工程的代建任务。"项目公司"原董事长陈永战、现董事长李祥、书记林光凯、项目经理惠丰等与纪念馆较为熟悉，知道他们是能干事、会干事、干成事的。他们接手后，招聘了玄武园林古建筑公司（以下简称"古建公司"）等修复施工单位，与"南大设计院"合作，在建筑群的科学保护上开动脑筋，提出了"危房变钢屋"的施工方案（民国建筑均为砖混结构，其寿命为 70 年左右，而利济巷的建筑已经 80 多年，其 8 幢小楼被有关部门定为险房，从下到上进行钢结构加固后，房屋和墙体的受重力转移至钢支架和混凝土地基上），特别是在以旧修旧上下足了功夫，仅在墙体外立面粉刷和门、窗油漆的工序上，曾经不仅反复研讨，而且在现场多次试验，不厌其烦地返工，直到取得各方满意的效果为止。他们还将整修过程中拆下的旧门旧窗、旧砖旧瓦、旧梁旧椽、旧物旧件，细心地保留下来，有的直接补充到房屋的修复中，有的移交给爱涛公司用于旧址遗物陈展，丰富了展览内容，增强了可看性。A 幢有一个楼梯立柱，就是从被拆下的废材料堆中找出，安装后发现，虽然有些细微裂痕，但旧物的恰当利用，为旧址陈列增色不少。因为大家有这样的共识，对于旧址修复工程来说，其建筑群和内外环境的塑造，本身就是重要的展陈现场，以旧修旧，往往正是检验旧址型陈列馆成功与否的关键所在。

四是精心塑造主题雕塑，找到了著名雕塑家吴显宁，委托其创作有关"慰安妇"的主题雕塑。吴显宁是无锡灵山大佛和山东曲阜孔子雕像等大型雕塑的设计师，也是纪念馆二期工程建设中《古城的灾难》组合雕塑，以及《历史证人的脚印》铜板路的设计师。他最初设计的"慰安妇"群雕体积较高大，裸露的较多，与现场的比例不够协调，后来我们在现场用木棍搭起了几个不同高度的框架，从不同的视角反复比较，定出合适的雕塑尺度。市委常委、宣传部长徐宁在审查雕塑底稿时提出，希望能够按照曾经在利济巷"东云慰安所"充当三年日军的性奴隶，后来又跟随日军转战到云南龙陵，成为孕妇出现在战壕里，并被中国军队救出的朝鲜籍"慰安妇"朴永心当年的历史照片为依据，重新创作一组"慰安妇"群雕。此后，我们又几次到位于江宁区方山艺术营的吴显宁工作室，反复修改琢磨，最后安装在利济巷慰安所旧址陈列馆的大门入口处，成为对现场具有震撼力的雕塑艺术作品，的确为整个展陈的效果增色不少。

五是特别重视邀请展陈团队，我们找到了江苏爱涛文化产业有限公司（以下简称"爱涛公司"），委托其展陈设计与制作。通过邀标的方式，请来三家专门的展陈艺术设计公司，经过专家评审，爱涛公司中标。该公司隶属于江苏省国有企业苏豪控股集团，算得上是国内一流的展览设计与制作专业公司，有过多项成功的业绩，曾经出色担纲或参与了多项国家级、省级博物馆的设计与制作，其中代表性的有上海世博会江苏馆、南京博物院、陕西历史博物馆、米兰世博会中国馆艺术品创作等项目。此次，他们以自己优秀的设计得以中标，但我认为他们在对于展馆特点、主旨内涵的把握上仍有偏差，所体现出的效果优美但忽略了与旧址风格的相协调，与我理想中的设计方案还有许多地方可以调整。因此，我要求他们先去附近的总统府和梅园新村纪念馆学习旧址陈列经验，然后重新设计，其方案经过多轮次的修改，最后才被采纳和通过。实践使我们体会到，一个好的艺术作品，一定要与场馆的风貌、环境特点和要表达的主题相协调，融为一体者为要为妙。

爱涛布展，优化特色"方案"

我始终坚信，不惧怕反复修改，自我的否定之否定，对于成就好作品是不可或缺的经历。在布展期间，我们与爱涛公司一起，经历了对旧址环境、氛围、格调不断磨合和调整的渐进过程。譬如说序厅的布展，其设计方案是两个不对称并呈现出一卷卷书状的薄钢板制品，上面刻着展览前言和诸多慰安所的名字，为了把握它的体量，安装到一个比较合适的位置上，爱涛公司先行做了同比例的木制模型，放置在现场一看，感到中间位置太小了，既不利于观众流畅地通行，也使得现场气势不足。我们在现场反复挪动模型，直到比例合适为止。制作成品后，又发现钢板上的文字用黑色字不够突出，又采用人工描写成为白色字前言。最后发现房屋上部比较空洞不够协调，又在四周增加一圈灰塑板，贴上国内外各个慰安所的历史照片，与下部钢板上的慰安所名字的文字相对应，使得上下呼应，层次错落，效果较好。再说展架、展板和文物柜样式，预前做了展览的支架结构和展板小样，挂在和摆放到展厅内，让大家评头论足。结果修改了多余的装饰性线条和不必要的底图，放大了说明的文字，加大了展板的尺寸，改变了展板悬挂的高度等，使得展架、展板与文物柜等展品，功能更好地与展厅的尺度、展品的色彩、展出的效果相协调，不留和少留遗憾。

利济巷的民国式二层小楼，原是国民党中将杨普庆于20世纪30年代陆续建造的私宅，主要用于居家和旅馆商住，房间狭小，楼道狭窄，一共有84间大大小小的房间，非常零碎，不太适合办馆，观众通行不畅，展陈流线和布局比想象中还要困难许多。为此，我们与爱涛公司、项目公司、南大设计院等有关人员，除了反复在图纸上作业，还多次在现场实地讨论，研究一幢一幢建筑物的特点，化解房间大小和形态不一难布局的难题，解决一层一层楼梯道难连接的困惑，为比选最佳方案不厌其烦，为求得最好的效果，多次推翻原方案重来。朝鲜籍"慰安妇"朴永心在利济巷现场指认的房间，无疑是展陈的重中之重。她的回忆中自己是住在利济巷2号楼二层的19号房间，在布展时将整座楼的30个房间，每个房间门口用一个小木牌标上房号，她所指认的房间正好是19号，现场验证了她受害经历证言的准确性。在时间紧、任务重、要求高的情况下，布展人员发扬不怕苦的精神，连续加班加点。记得有一天，从下午1点开始，我会同纪念馆几位年轻的学者袁志秀、曹林、孙红亮、张国松、刘广建等，与爱涛公司陈国欢总经理、陈思宁副总经理和任睿、高伦、周紫金、赵烽晨、朱春梅、王斯元、陶晓杰、陈西铭、江燕、宋颂、孙莹、邱莹、李涛等设计师与施工人员，在利济巷旧址的一幢幢小楼里，一间间展室过堂，一件件展品调整，就这么进进出出，上上下下，走走停停，走着转着，边转边议，边议边调，直到晚上 8 时 30 分结束，整整耗费 7 个半小时，大家没有坐下休息一分钟。完成后，才感到腰酸腿痛，身疲力竭，但没有人喊苦叫累。正是有了这种敬业、精细的意识和不怕苦累的精神，才使得展陈方案在布展施工的过程中不断被优化，变旧址陈列的劣势为优势，一个个展陈亮点被陆续发掘和展示出来。

以泪为魂，塑造精神空间

在我们对利济巷旧址陈列布展的过程中，始终在思考能否找到一个类似《人类的浩劫——侵华日军南京大屠杀史实展》中"12 秒"（如果把南京大屠杀经历的六个星期时间以秒来计算，并除以 30 万死难者的数字，平均每 12 秒就有一条生命消失）的点睛之笔，能够给观众留下久久不能忘记的创意。然而，这个神来之笔往往又不容易找准和找到。

一天凌晨，我在家修改利济巷外景观方案时，脑海中突然冒出"泪"的设想。我仿佛看见，当年许许多多"慰安妇"抹着眼泪，曾经泪洒利济巷慰安所的墙上、路上、地上，虽然随着时间的推移，她们的泪已干，但好像在旧址里并未消失。沿着这条思路，我想到了以"泪"为一条主线，来串起这里的内外展览，以泪为魂，形成特色。于是，我设想在外景展区刻意设立泪洒一面墙（泪墙）、泪滴一条路（泪路）、泪湿一块地（泪地），在展厅内的基本陈列尾厅里设立"流不尽的泪"（泪流），即塑造一尊"慰安妇"幸存者的半身铜像，安装在墙上。那天早晨，我将这些设想以短信的方式发给了徐宁部长，向她汇报，没想到很快得到领导的赞同，说给我一个大大的"赞"！不仅如此，南大设计院、项目公司、爱涛公司一致赞成我的这个创意，大家都在考虑这些泪滴如何实现的方式，争取最好的效果。

南大设计院与古建公司负责对"泪路"的设计，他们将利济巷慰安所旧址内楼与楼之间道路上的窨井盖子上阴刻有一大两小"三滴泪"，既在一定程度上美化了馆内路上众多的窨井盖，又使窨井盖具有方向性，成为外展区指路牌。项目公司和爱涛公司合作建设"泪地"，爱涛公司用铝塑板制作了展馆入口处一面墙上几十张"慰安妇"幸存者的面孔，项目公司则在那堵墙下的一块地上，暗装了自动喷水系统，使那块地始终保持潮湿状态。在展馆入口处迎面墙上，爱涛公司负责做泪滴，但用什么去做，做成什么形状，多大的体积为好，一时间都没有可参考的标准。后来，他们先用玻璃球做成了"泪滴"，我觉得除了用透明的玻璃材质效果较好外，体积显得太小，还感到形状不够理想。后来我在洋河酒瓶商标上得到启发，给"泪滴"加一个长长的"泪线"，效果一下出来了，而且我们决定尽量放大"泪滴"尺度，对其进行夸张性的艺术处理，使之产生震撼的效果。

如果说外景展区的三处"泪滴"只是给观众一个印象、一个铺垫、一个伏笔的话，展厅内的两处"泪滴"则是点明主题、高度概括、集中提炼，更应该精心做好。实事求是地说，序厅里的"无言的泪团"（泪团）在原设计方案中是没有的，爱涛公司的设计师们在厅中间的屋顶部垂下一团铁丝网，网里面横七竖八地挂着大大小小的"慰安妇"幸存者的照片，显得凌乱，而且这样的陈展方式对幸存者们也不够尊重。我建议他们用细钢筋扎成一个个圆圈，上面挂满"慰安妇"幸存者的照片，并且圆圈越向下越小，照片则越向上越大，最后收缩到中间，变成"泪团"。由于时间来不及，他们先用有机玻璃块代替，开馆后再用玻璃制作成圆形状的"泪团"，悬挂在观众的头顶上，形成强烈的震撼力。尾厅里的"流不尽的泪"的雕塑像初稿设计并不理想，其形象做得太美了。我提出要选一张布满岁月沧桑"慰安妇"幸存者的脸来做原型，并且让其眼眶里一直噙着泪花，让观众去帮助拭去眼泪，形成互动。最后，选定林石姑那张带有痛苦、悲怆、皱纹密布的脸，在雕像的眼眶后面穿了两个小洞，用一台微型小水泵，并安装上调控水流的开关，其效果得到观众广泛的认可和称赞，成为该馆展陈中最大的亮点。中国人民抗日战争纪念馆原副馆长于延俊在参观利济巷慰安妇旧址陈列馆后评价说："当我给老妈妈擦拭眼泪时，她的眼角里流出了眼泪，我边擦也跟着流泪了。"她评价整个展陈是"创新，震撼，令人耳目一新"。

个人简介

朱成山

汉族，1954年7月生，
中共党员，江苏南京人，
中共江苏省委外宣办原副主任，
侵华日军南京大屠杀遇难同胞纪念馆原馆长，
中国抗日战争史学会副会长，
中国博物馆协会陈列艺术专业委员会副主任、研究员。

PREFACE

TO STORE THEIR MEMORIES IN THIS MEMORIAL HALL OF TEARS

On December 1st, 2015, Nanjing Museum of Site of Lijixiang Comfort Stations officially opened to the public, so far as the largest and most intact architectural complex of Japanese military "comfort houses" in Asia and beyond. Many official leaders attended the opening ceremony, including Cui Yuying, the vice minister of the Propaganda Department of the Central Committee of the CPC and the deputy director of the State Council Information Office ; Wang Yanwen, member of Jiangsu Provincial Standing Committee and the director of the Propaganda Department ; Xu Ning, member of the Nanjing Municipal Standing Committee and the director of the Propaganda Department . Many medias reported extensively on the event, such as Xinhua News Agency, China News Service, Xinhua Daily, Yangtse Evening Post and Nanjing Daily and so on, spreading this news to people around the country. As the planner, participant, administrator and the one in charge of this project, I can still remember every detail of the construction progress. These memories are coming back to me, vividly and freshly, like they all happened yesterday.

AFTER ALL THE TWISTS AND TURNS, I TOOK CHARGE OF THE CONSTRUCTION WORK

People are meant to do what the destiny has arranged. Believe it or not, whenever a special bond occurs between you and the certain task, you can never cut it off. The story of how I became the project director in charge of constructing the Nanjing Museum of Site of Lijixiang Comfort Stations is a typical example for this very truth.
When the site of former "comfort house" in Lijixiang was still under the administration of Baixia District, the then district mayor, Cao Yongning, came to me one day and told me his plan about this site. Lijixiang is located at Changbaijie, a significant historic conservation area in planning, and there are eight two-story buildings of brick-wood structure built during the time of the Republic of China (1912-1949) left unoccupied since the housing demolition in 2008. Close to the buildings is the Kexiang food market. The whole site was in a bad condition, with garbage piling up and buildings seriously damaged, which really disfigured the beauty of the city. For this reason, the government of Baixia District decided to make a restoration and build this site into a memorial hall of "comfort house" . After then, with an adjustment of administrative divisions, the area where the site is located is now under the administration of Qinhuai District. The then first deputy chief, Xue Fengguan, asked me to be their history consultant for the memorial hall construction, to which I gladly agreed. The municipal leaders of Nanjing had assigned the whole project to the Bureau of Culture, Broadcasting, Television, Press and Publication, but the deputy director of the Bureau, Yan Yiping, came to me for support, and I found no reason to reject such a request. Out of surprise, after experiencing all the twists and turns, the municipal leaders delegated this restoration project directly to me and made it clear that it would be run as a branch of The Memorial Hall of the Victims in Nanjing Massacre by Japanese Invaders. To be honest, as the curator of the Memorial Hall, I was busy in an extension project of building a new exhibition hall themed as "Victory".

Besides, as the hall was applying for the "World Memory Heritage" and preparing for the first national memorial day, there was a quite load of work for me to do, so I politely declined their request. However, the major leaders of Nanjing Municipal Party Committee and government both criticized and encouraged me by saying that they were all busy and being busy is a good thing. They said the project could be entrusted to a construction company and I would preside over their work.

With their trust, I took this important mission of restoring the site of the former "comfort house" in Lijixiang when I was already overloaded with working tasks in October, 2014.

TO RESTORE OLD BUILDINGS TO ITS OLD-FASHION BEAUTY: THE CREATION OF A QUALITY PROJECT

It probably has something to do with my 20 years' life in the army that I always exert myself to the utmost to accomplish my missions well.

After I undertook the task of this project, I fulfill it in five aspects:

First of all, I paid a visit to professor Zhao Chen and Leng Tian in the Institute of Architecture Design & Planning of Nanjing University (hereafter referred to as "the Institute"), and commissioned them to come up with a design scheme of the restoration project in Lijixiang as soon as possible. Actually, in the meetings held in Baixia and Qinhuai Districts to discuss about the restoration project, I had heard their design and given my opinion. Although I was only serving as a supporting part at that time, I acquired some knowledge of their design concept and basic orientation, which made it easier for me to follow up their plan. After Hou Shuguang, the deputy curator of the Memorial Hall, and I explained our intention, they immediately agreed to help. Their scheme soon got approved by the municipal leaders and the relevant department. What's more, during the construction period, we worked hard in cooperation to revise the design again and again and put our heads together to better the project. We studied and researched this project as an academic practice, in which we both gave full play to our strengths and became reliable working partners. It should be highlighted that the architectural art and exhibition art are inseparably interconnected in memorial halls, especially in those exhibition halls built on the site of old buildings. In other words, with an architectural design lacking unique artistic features, the exhibition art will have no foothold and cannot fully develop its charm.

Secondly, I quickly organized a team to write the outlines of the exhibition and display. The young scholars I picked up for this reason were asked to finish the script of the exhibition as soon as possible. Considering the actual situation of the new exhibition room themed as "Victory" in the memorial hall, and also with the intention of providing new researchers of the Memorial Hall with an opportunity to prove their worthiness, I chose four youngsters to undertake this task, including Yuan Zhixiu, the deputy director of the research storage department; Cao Lin, the deputy chief of the research department; and Zhang Guosong and Liu Guangjian, graduate students of the research department. The deputy chief of the storage department, Sun Hongliang, and Qin Yi as well as some other graduate students were commissioned to select relevant cultural relics for the display. I presided over all their work and revised the drafts. After discussions, it was decided that the exhibition hall would be divided into six parts, with one for basic exhibition, one for relic exhibition, and four for themed exhibitions. Small buildings located in Area A are used for basic exhibition: Sexual Slaves in WW Ⅱ —The Japanese Military "Comfort Women" System and Its Crimes. The buildings in Area B are used to display relics discovered in the sites of the former "comfort houses" named as "The Nightmare of Jinling—Japanese Military 'Comfort Houses' in Nanjing and the 'Comfort Women' ". Four buildings in Area C are used for themed exhibitions, respectively named as "Tears of Sex Slaves in Shanghai—The Exhibition on the Crime Evidences of Japanese Military 'Comfort Women' System from the 'Comfort Houses' in Shanghai", "Japanese Military 'Comfort Houses' Scattered all over China—The Miserable Memories of Chinese 'Comfort Women' ", "Painful Memory and Denouncement—The Exhibition on History Facts of 'Comfort Women' from Korean" Peninsula, and "The Sex Slaves from Different Countries—The Historical Facts of Sexual Slaves in the Pacific War and the Crimes of Japanese Military 'Comfort

Women's System". Upon determining the structure, we divided the work. The young scholars went separately to look for relevant documentaries, and they were responsible for searching for pictures and relics as well as writing the exhibition explanations. They would send me their results for revision and approval. If finding them unsatisfying, I would send them back for an improvement. After several rounds of revisions and amendments, the outline was approaching perfection. Later, I invited some experts to review our outline again and asked them for advice, among whom there were professor Su Zhiliang from Shanghai Normal University, professor Jing Shenghong from Nanjing Normal University, professor Zhao Chen from the Institute, and Chen Yongzhan, the chief engineer of Urban Construction Group. At last, the final draft was sent to the relevant department and leaders for approval. The outline of the exhibition and display, with its unique features, was finally determined.

Thirdly, I received an order to find an engineering company for the project, so I selected Nanjing Urban Construction Project Construction Management Co. (hereafter referred to as the construction company) to be our construction agency. Although the project was defined as confidential, it could be entrusted to the construction company. But why did I choose this specific construction company among all others? It is simply because the company has rich experience in the construction of large-scale projects, like Nanjing Railway Station, Nanjing South Railway Station, and some projects in Mofanmalu and Longpanlu. It is an excellent cooperator that is able to conquer any difficulties to accomplish their work. In addition, the construction company has done an impressive job in the second-stage extension project of the Memorial Hall. The former chairman of the company Chen Yongzhan, its current chairman Li Xiang, the company's communist party secretary Lin Guangkai, and the project manager Hui Feng are all familiar with the Memorial Hall. I deem it as a reliable, competent and responsible company. After taking this job, they hired the Xuanwu Landscape and Traditional Chinese Architectural Engineering Company (hereafter referred to as "Traditional Chinese Architectural Engineering Company") to do the repairing work, and cooperated with the Institute to devise a plan of repairing the dilapidated buildings by using steels as a protection to the old building complex. It should be noted that constructions built during the period of the Republic of China are of brick-wood structure with a lifespan of 70 years. The buildings in Lijixiang have been standing there for more than 80 years, 8 of which have been testified as dilapidated buildings by the relevant department. Using steel structures to reinforce the buildings, the stress the buildings and their walls were enduring was transferred to the steel structures and the concrete foundations. What's more, they also made much effort not to damage the old fashion of these buildings. Take the process of painting the outer walls, doors and windows for example, they discussed the procedure again and again, carried out a lot of experiments on the construction sites and didn't mind remaking the paints again and again until the results satisfied everyone. They even reserved things they removed from the buildings during the restoration, including the old doors, windows, bricks, tiles, roof beams, rafters and so on. Some of these old things have been used in the restored buildings, while the others were handed over to Artall Company for the exhibition of relics, which adds the content of the exhibition, making it more worth-seeing. A staircase column installed in building A is a good example of recycling the dismantled parts. After installing it into the building, we find that although there are some hairline cracks on the column, it adds charms to the exhibition of relics. It is agreed that the decoration both inside and outside the buildings is also an important part of the exhibition. To restore an old building to its old fashion plays an essential part in the success of a memorial hall built in the historic sites.

Fourthly, we came to the famous sculptor, Wu Xianning, and invited him to create a theme sculpture of "comfort women" for the memorial hall. Wu Xianning is the designer of many large-scale sculptures, including the famous Lingshan Buddha in Wuxi and the statue of Confucius in Qufu, Shandong. He also designed the combination sculpture "Disaster of the Old City" for the second-stage extension project of the memorial hall and the copper plate road "the Footprints of the Historical Witnesses". The first version of the combination sculpture of "comfort women" was too large and showed too much nudity, not matching its surroundings. So we used wooden sticks to build up some frames of different heights and put them on the spot. After comparing these frames from different angles, we finally found the proper size of the sculpture. Xu Ning, member of the Standing Committee of the

Municipal Party Committee and the director of the Propaganda Department, reviewed the sculpture manuscript and suggested that it should be recreated based on the picture of Pak Young Sim, a "comfort woman" taken by the Japanese soldier from Korea to China. She was once forced into sexual slavery by Japanese soldiers for three years in "Dongyun Comfort House" in Lijixiang. The picture was taken in a trench of Longling, Yunnan, where she got pregnant and rescued by Chinese army. Later, we paid several visits to Wu Xianning's studio located at the Fangshan Arts Camp in Jiangning District and revised the manuscript again and again. Now you can see a sculpture standing at the entrance of the relic exhibition hall, exciting the mind of every visitor and truly enhancing the exhibition effect.

Fifthly, we invited three professional exhibition design companies for bid. After the appraisal and evaluation of experts, the Artall Cultural Industry Co. Ltd (hereafter referred to as "Artall company") won the bidding, and was entrusted with the design and execution of the exhibitions. It is affiliated with the Soho Holding Group Corp. Ltd, a state-owned corporation in Jiangsu, and is a first-class exhibition company at home. Artall company has performed impressively in its past projects. For example, it played an important role in the design and execution of both state and provincial museums. Its representative projects include the Jiangsu Pavilion in Shanghai World Expo, Nanjing Museum, Shaanxi History Museum, and the artworks displayed in the Chinese Pavilion in Milan World Expo. Although their great design had won them the bidding, I thought they didn't exactly grasp the characteristics and theme of our memorial hall. Their design presented a beautiful scene, but it could not harmonize with the style of the site. I thought there is much room for improvement before it reached my ideal standards. Therefore, I told them to learn from the successful design experience of Presidential Palace and Memorial of Meiyuan New Village and redesign their scheme. It went through many rounds of modifications before being accepted. From this experience, we learn that a good artwork must go with the style, characteristics and theme of the exhibition hall. It is important for them to integrate into one.

TO IMPROVE EXHIBITS ARRANGEMENT WITH ARTALL

I always adhere to the idea that repeated modifications are necessary before a fine work is finally created. During the period of arranging the exhibits, it takes us a lot of efforts to make adjustments so that our exhibition can best harmonize with the surroundings, atmosphere and style of the site of the former "comfort houses". Take the arrangements in preface hall for example, the design scheme is to make scroll-like walls with thin steel plates, on which writes the preface of the exhibition and the names of those "comfort houses". In order to produce these walls in right size and install them in the right location, the Artall Company firstly made a wooden model of the same size and put it on the right center of the hall. We found that it would hinder visitors from passing and weaken the power of heart-shaking. So we kept moving the model until we finally found its most suitable location. Later, the words on its finished product turned out to be not prominent enough in black, so we manually repainted them into white. After all these were done, there came another problem. The upper space of the hall was too empty to go with the exhibitions, so circles of grey plastic plates were hung on the roof, showing historic pictures of "comfort houses" both at home and abroad, which correspond to the names written on the steel plates below. With the designs echoing with each other, a structured space with a good visual effect was finally created. Another example I want to mention is the adjustments we made on the display racks, panels and showcases of the cultural relics. We first put some display racks and panel samples in the exhibition hall for people to comment on. Based on their suggestions, we made some modifications to the panels, such as removing the unnecessary decorative lines and images, enlarging the panels and the words on them as well as increasing their hanging height, which make exhibition items like the display racks, panels and showcases better match the dimensions, colors and effects of the exhibition hall. We tried our best to finish this task with less or even no regrets left.

The two-story buildings built during the period of the Republic of China in Lijixiang were originally the private mansion of Yang Puqing, a lieutenant general of Kuomintang. They were finished one by one in the 1930s. They were used as living houses or hotels, with small rooms and narrow corridors. There are 84 rooms with different sizes in these buildings, which kind of layout made these buildings unsuitable to be used as exhibition hall, since it may hinder visitors from walking around freely. Therefore, we encountered much more difficulties in designing the routes and layouts of exhibitions. Working with the professionals and experts from the Artall company, the construction company and the Institute, we studied this problem both on the blueprint and on the spot. We researched the features of these buildings and found solutions to the problems caused both by differences in room sizes and shapes and by the connection of floors. We tirelessly compared different solutions, aiming to find the best one, during which we gave up the selected schemes and started again for many times. The room identified by the former "comfort woman" Pak Young Sim is unquestionably one of the most important part for the exhibition. She remembered that she lived in the Room 19 on the second floor of Building 2 in Lijixiang. When arranging the exhibits, we marked rooms' numbers on wooden plates on the doors. After marking all the 30 rooms in that building, we found that the one she identified was No.19, which proved the truth of her testimony. Since we needed to do so many things with high requirements in such limited time, people responsible for exhibition arrangements were keeping over-working continuously, never complaining about being tired or the hardships. I can still recall a day of such experience. On that day, I was touring each exhibition room with a bunch of people, including several young scholars working in the memorial hall, namely Yuan Zhixiu, Cao Lin, Sun Hongliang, Zhang Guosong, Liu Guangjian; the general manager of the Artall company, Chen Guohuan; its deputy general manager, Chen Sining; and some other designers and workers, namely Ren Rui, Gao Lun, Zhou Zijin, Zhao Fengchen, Zhu Chunmei, Wang Siyuan, Tao Xiaojie, Chen Ximing, Jiang Yan, Song Song, Sun Ying, Qiu Ying, Li Tao and so on. We checked each exhibit and made adjustments whenever it was necessary. Climbing up and down, walking and discussing, we worked non-stop for over 7 hours from 1 p.m. to 8:30 p.m. We hadn't felt exhausted until we finished the tour, but no one made any complaint. We all devoted ourselves to the work, and always paid attention to the details. It was with this spirit that we managed to improve our exhibition schemes during the construction period, and find out every highlight of our exhibitions by transferring the disadvantages of the exhibition on the historical site to our advantageous features.

TO REPRODUCE THE INNER WORLD OF "COMFORT WOMEN" WITH THE TEARS

During the exhibition arrangements in Lijixiang, we were trying to figure out a creative idea which can help to raise the whole design to a higher level, and we were searching for a similar effect created in the design of "12 seconds" shown in the exhibition of Nanjing Massacre by Japanese Invaders. If 300,000, the number of people killed in the Nanjing Massacre, is divided by the time in seconds (the massacre lasted for 6 weeks), the result tells us that in every 12 seconds one life was taken during that massacre. The idea of "12 seconds" leaves a deep impression in the heart of visitors. An idea like this can inspire visitors to think more deeply about the exhibition, but it is hard to find one pertinent to our exhibition theme.
One morning, when I was revising the design scheme of the outer-door scene, the idea of teardrop suddenly came to my mind. I saw a vision that a lot of "comfort women" were wiping away their tears, which dropped on the walls, roads, grounds of the "comfort houses" in Lijixiang. Although the tears have dried away with the time, they are still there in the site of the former "comfort houses". Holding to this idea, I thought it could be our feature to use "teardrop" as a mainline to connect all the exhibitions both inside and outside together. Therefore, we established a wall, a road and a ground of tears to demonstrate that this was a place where all the "comfort women" once shed their tears. At the end of the basic exhibition hall, we displayed a bronze bust of a "comfort woman" installed on the wall, named as "The Endless Tears". On that morning I sent a message to Xu Ning, the director of the Propaganda Department, reporting to her about my idea. Out of surprise, she immediately approved it and told me she really liked this idea. What's more, the Institute, the construction Company and Artall company were all in

favor of it. They all tried their best to find ways to realize this idea to reach its best effect.

The Institute and the Traditional Chinese Architectural Engineering Company worked together to deign the "road of tears". On the ground among the buildings, there are many manhole covers. Each cover is incised with a design of "three teardrops", with one drop larger than the others. This design helps to beautify the manhole covers in the memorial hall, and the three teardrops can also direct the way to the outer-door exhibitions. The construction company and the Artall company cooperated to build the "ground of tears". The Artall company put an aluminium-plastic panel on a wall located at the entrance to the exhibition hall, on which there are dozens of pictures of the "comfort women" survivors. On the ground below the wall, a concealed automatic water sprinkler system was installed by the construction company to maintain the wetness of the ground. The Artall company was also responsible to create some teardrop-like design on a outer-wall of the exhibition hall that faces the entrance. In the first place, they had no clue how to make the "teardrops", and were uncertain about the shape, size, or material for this design. Later, they used glass balls as the "teardrops". Although glass can present a good transparent effect, the size and shape of those balls were unsatisfactory. I was inspired by the brand design on a Yanghe Wine bottle and added to the glass ball a long "trail of teardrop", which looked really like a teardrop then. We also enlarged its size as big as possible, whose artistic exaggeration effect makes them more heart-shocking.

If the design of "three teardrops" on the outer-door exhibition area only serves as a foreshadowing for visitors to understand our theme, the designs inside the exhibition halls are the ones that should really point out the idea. In this case, we put more efforts into this task. To be honest, the design of "silent tears" was missed in the original scheme. At first, the Artall company planned to hung a ball of iron wires over the central part of the roof, with pictures of the "comfort women" survivors in the wire net. I thought the pictures would look like a mess, showing no respect to the survivors, so I suggested they should hung those pictures in the frames made of thin steel wires, with the sizes of the frames getting smaller when they are getting closer to the ground. These pictures are then grouped in the shape of a large drop of tears. As time was limited, they first used organic glass as an alternate, and later changed them to round-shape "teardrops" with glass and suspended them over the head of visitors, producing a strong power of heart-quivering. There is a bust named "endless tears" installed in the end of the exhibition hall. The first design of it was unsuitably beautiful. I proposed that we should select a "comfort woman" that has a look of having been through vicissitudes of life as the prototype of the bust, and keep the eyes of the bust shedding tears all the time, creating an interaction for visitors to help wipe away the tears. At last, we chose Lin Shigu's wrinkled and sorrowful face as the prototype of the design. There are two small holes in the eyes of the bust, with a micro pump controlled by a water flow regulator. Its effect has been widely praised by the visitors and has become the biggest highlight in the exhibition hall. Yu Yanjun, the former deputy curator of the Museum of the War of Chinese People's Resistance Against Japanese Aggression made her comment after the visit and said, "When I was wiping away the tears on the old lady's face, I saw her tears keep coming down from her eyes, and it made me fail to hold back mine." She appraised the whole exhibition as "creative, overwhelming, and refreshing".

Personal Profile
Zhu Chengshan,
Han, born in July 1954,
member of CPC, from Nanjing, Jiangsu,
former deputy director of Foreign Affairs Office of Jiangsu Province,
former curator of The Memorial Hall of the Victims in Nanjing Massacre by Japanese Invaders,
deputy director of Chinese Society for the History of War against Japanese Aggression,
deputy director and researcher of Chinese Museum Association Exhibition Art Specialized Committee.

NANJING MUSEUM
OF SITE OF LIJIXIANG

目 录 CATALOG COMFORT STATIONS
ART ATLAS EXHIBIT

展览概况
General Situation of the Exhibition Site

▶ 1

刻血泪历史之殇
承捍卫正义之责
Keeping in Mind Historical Tragedy and Taking on the Responsibility of Safeguarding Justice

▶ 6

设计的情感
Feeling of Design

▶ 10

设计团队
Designing Team

▶ 14

室外展陈
Outdoor Exhibition

▶ 17

室内展陈
Indoor Exhibition

▶ 27

建设历程
The Construction Process

▶ 139

媒体报道摘录
Media Reports Extract

▶ 153

公司荣誉
Glories

▶ 158

展 览 概 况

GENERAL SITUATION OF
THE EXHIBITION SITE

南京利济巷慰安所旧址，由原国民党中将杨普庆于1935—1937年间陆续建造，为两层砖木混合结构的建筑物，名为"普庆新村"。1937年底，日军占领南京之后，将利济巷2号改造为"东云慰安所"，将18号改造为"故乡楼慰安所"。其中，利济巷2号楼上第19号房间是朝鲜籍"慰安妇"朴永心当年被拘禁的地方。2003年11月21日，她曾经来现场进行指认。利济巷成为唯一经在世的外籍慰安妇指认的慰安所。2014年11月，市政府启动对利济巷慰安所旧址的修缮保护、陈列布展工作。2015年5月1日，利济巷慰安所旧址修缮改造工程正式开工建设。

Nanjing Museum of Site of Lijixiang Comfort Stations used to be a two-story wooden and brick building built by former Kuomintang lieutenant general Yang Puqing from 1935 to 1937. It was originally named "Puqing Xin Cun", or "Puqing New Village". At the end of 1937, after Japanese troops occupied Nanjing, they transformed No.2 Lijixiang into "Dongyun Comfort House" and No.18 into "Guxianglou Comfort House". Room No.19 of Building No.2 in Lijixiang was the place where Pak Young Sim, a Korean "comfort woman" was imprisoned. On November 21, 2003, she came to identify the site, making Lijixiang the only "comfort house" that has been identified by the surviving foreign "comfort woman". In November 2014, Nanjing municipal government launched restoration and exhibition project for Lijixiang "Comfort House" Site and the project officially opened on May 1, 2015.

利济巷慰安所旧址陈列馆全景图

展览概况　GENERAL SITUATION OF THE EXHIBITION SITE

2003年11月21日,朴永心老人来到自己曾经度过三年非人生活的日军慰安所(现南京利济巷2号)时回忆说,她当年的日本名字叫"歌丸",在日军慰安所门前,朴永心禁不住失声痛哭。

朴永心现场指认图

2015年12月1日"南京利济巷慰安所旧址陈列馆"举办开馆仪式,作为侵华日军南京大屠杀遇难同胞纪念馆(以下称"纪念馆")的分馆,这里是亚洲地区最大、保存最完整的一处日军慰安所旧址。陈列馆由8幢淡黄色的两层建筑组成,占地约3680平方米,展陈面积约3000平方米。此次陈列分为基本陈列、旧址陈列和4个专题陈列,包括"'二战'中的性奴隶""金陵梦魇""沪城性奴泪""遍布中国的日军慰安所""伤痛记忆与控诉""众多国籍的性奴隶",全面介绍了侵华日军"慰安妇"制度的起源、确立与灭亡过程,中国、朝鲜半岛、东南亚及太平洋诸岛等地的慰安所,以及遗留的侵华日军"慰安妇"问题与相关历史记忆,共展出照片680多张,文物1600多件,视频19部。

On December 1, 2015, Nanjing exhibition hall of Site of Lijixiang Comfort Stations was opened to the public. As a branch of the Memorial Hall of the Victims in Nanjing Massacre by Japanese Invaders (hereafter referred to as Memorial Hall), it is the biggest and best preserved Japanese "comfort house" site. The exhibition hall is composed of eight yellowish two-story buildings, covering an area of 3,680 square meters, while the exbition area is 3,000 square meters. This exhibition consists of basic exhibition, site exhibition and four feature exhibitions, including "Sexual Slaves in WWII", "The Nightmare of Jinling", "Tears of Sex Slaves in Shanghai", "Japanese Military Comfort Houses Scattered all over China", "Painful Memory and Denouncement" and "Sex Slaves from Various Nations". They illustrated the origin, the establishment and the fall of Japanese invaders' "comfort women" system, described "comfort houses" in China, Korean Peninsula, Southeast Asia and various islands on Pacific Ocean, and demonstrated historical memories related to survived "comfort women". More than 680 photos, 1,600 pieces of relics and 19 videos are exhibited here.

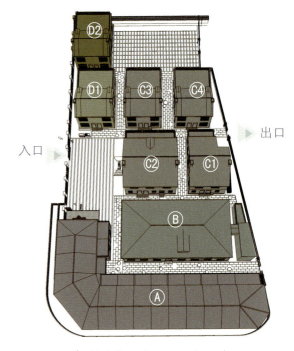

| 利济巷旧址平面示意图 |

A区(基本陈列)
"二战"中的性奴隶
——日军"慰安妇"制度及其罪行展

B区(旧址陈列)
金陵梦魇
——南京日军慰安所与"慰安妇"史实展

C区(专题陈列)
C1 沪城性奴泪
——上海慰安所与日军"慰安妇"制度罪证展

C2 遍布中国的日军慰安所
——中国"慰安妇"血泪记忆展

C3 伤痛记忆与控诉
——来自朝鲜半岛的日军"慰安妇"受害史实展

C4 众多国籍的性奴隶
——太平洋战争与日军"慰安妇"制度罪行展

D1 办公区

D2 馆藏区

| 展览概况 GENERAL SITUATION OF THE EXHIBITION SITE |

一层流线图

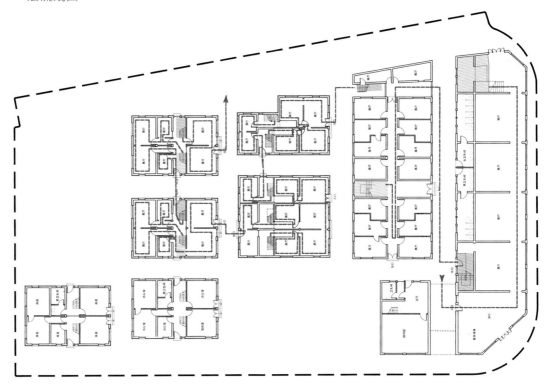

二层流线图

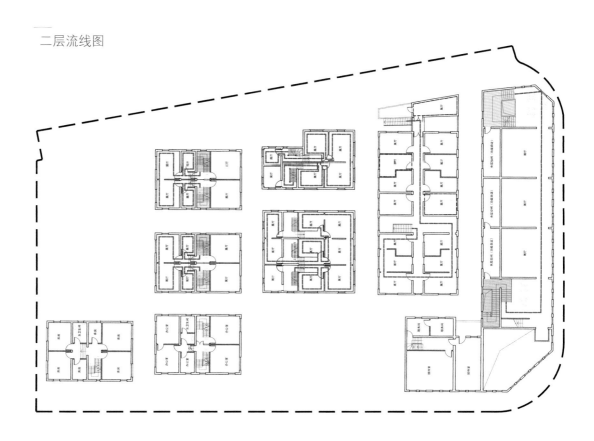

刻血泪历史之殇，承捍卫正义之责
——记南京利济巷慰安所旧址陈列展览设计

KEEPING IN MIND HISTORICAL TRAGEDY AND TAKING ON THE RESPONSIBILITY OF SAFEGUARDING JUSTICE
——PREFACE TO THE EXHIBITION DESIGN FOR NANJING MUSEUM OF SITE OF LIJIXIANG COMFORT STATIONS

1937年日本帝国主义悍然发动了对中国的侵略战争，侵略者的铁蹄践踏了祖国的河山，流离失所的人们在沦陷的国土上苦苦挣扎。在万千遭受苦难的同胞中，还有"慰安妇"这样一个并不为人所熟知的特殊群体：她们被日本军国主义以欺骗、掳掠、强迫等手段，强行征召，被迫为日本军人提供性服务、充当性奴隶。在此期间，她们受到了心理和生理的双重迫害和摧残。而在战后漫长的时间内，那段沉重、痛苦的记忆，并没有随着战争的结束而停止，更成为她们挥之不去的梦魇，泪水伴随她们的一生。

70年前，中国人民经过长达八年的艰苦卓绝的斗争，取得了中国人民抗日战争的伟大胜利，宣告了世界反法西斯战争的完全胜利，和平的阳光再次普照大地。这是正义战胜邪恶、光明战胜黑暗、进步战胜反动的伟大胜利。

In 1937, the Japanese empire launched an aggressive war towards China. The troops of the aggressor trod on our homeland and forced many of our people into homelessness and suffering. Among our countless long-suffering compatriots, there was a special group called "comfort women" who have remained generally unfamiliar to the public. These women were pushed into sex slavery by a combination of deceit, kidnapping and coercion. During this time, they suffered both mentally and physically. However, those painful memories didn't vanish with the end of the war. They have haunted the women throughout the rest of their lives, and tears of sadness have been with them ever since.

Seventy years ago, the Chinese defeated the Japanese Aggression after eight years of bitter fighting, marking the end of the worldwide struggle against fascism. Since then, the sunshine of peace has shone across the globe. This was a victory of justice overcoming evil, brightness overcoming darkness, and civilization overcoming aggression.

70年后，在中国人民抗日战争和世界反法西斯战争胜利70周年之际，南京利济巷慰安所旧址陈列馆项目其中所承载的那段鲜为人知的血泪史及其所蕴含的意义就显得那样特殊并且尤为重要。利济巷日军慰安所旧址陈列馆系原国民党中将杨普庆于1935—1937年建造的高级"洋房"，日军占领南京后，将利济巷2号改造为"东云慰安所"，将18号改造为"故乡楼慰安所"，为在宁的日军官兵提供罪恶的慰安服务。利济巷目前是亚洲地区最大、保存最完整的一处日军慰安所旧址，是唯一一处被在世外籍慰安妇指认过的慰安所建筑，是中国大陆第一座以"慰安妇"为主题的纪念馆。

Today, on the seventieth anniversary of victory against Japanese aggression, and the completion of the world anti-fascist war, the items exhibited in Nanjing Museum of Site of Lijixiang Comfort Stations bear great significance because of the tragic history behind them.
Lijixiang Comfort House Site used to be Kuomintang lieutenant general Yang Puqing's fancy foreign-style house, which was built from 1935 to 1937. After Japanese troops occupied Nanjing, they transformed No.2 Lijixiang into "Dongyun Comfort House" and No.18 into "Guxianglou Comfort House". These two Houses became the places where sex services were provided for Japanese soldiers. Lijixiang Comfort House Site is currently the biggest and best-preserved site of Japanese "comfort houses" in Asia and is also the only "comfort house" building that has been identified by surviving comfort women in person. It is the first "comfort women" themed museum in mainland China.

| 展览概况　GENERAL SITUATION OF THE EXHIBITION SITE |

忘记历史就意味着背叛，否认罪责就意味着重犯，将这段不为人知的历史往事客观真实地呈现于世人面前，是对于军国主义分子企图罔顾侵略战争历史，推卸历史罪责态度的警惕与反对；是对于在战争中，中国女性乃至世界各国女性所遭受的苦难历史的铭记；也是对于已经逝去或依然幸存的受害者们最深的告慰，是为了让人们牢记历史，谴责日军违反人权和道义的罪行，更是为了让人们以史为鉴，珍爱和平，开创未来。

因此，从投入该项目工作的第一天起，公司上下便全员明确思想，统一认识：此次利济巷慰安所旧址陈列展览项目与以往所参与的文化项目有着极大的不同，兼具文化价值、社会价值、历史价值与政治意义，是一个极其严肃的政治任务。因为其主题的特殊性与敏感性，不仅政府高度重视，社会高度关注，更是受到海内外各方人士的瞩目。所以我们的每一个想法、每一个创意，都需要经得起历史的检验与推敲。整个团队都深切地感受到社会各界的灼灼目光，意识到肩上的责任重如泰山。最终，参与项目的所有人员都认识到要以尊重历史为前提，将让历史说话，用史实发言作为根本出发点，以精诚之心待之，以审慎之思处之。

Forgetting history is a form of betrayal, and denying the existence of a crime can lead to that crime being repeated. Showing this unknown history truthfully is a warning and protest against the fact that militarists still attempt to deny the aggressive war history and shirk historic blame and responsibility. It is maintained in memory of the suffering that Chinese women and women around the world went through, and also to console the deceased and the survivors of the war. It aims at allowing people to keep history in mind and at condemning Japanese troops' crimes against rights and basic morality. It also enables us to learn lessons from history, cherish peace and build a better future.

Therefore, from the first day of the project, all the team members involved have worked with a common understanding that the Nanjing Museum of Site of Lijixiang Comfort Stations project is quite different from those cultural projects they have previously participated in. This is because this project is involved with cultural, social, historical and political values, which makes it a solemn political task. Since its theme is very special and sensitive, not only have the Chinese government and the whole society attached great importance to it, but people from all walks of life, at home and abroad, have fixed their eyes on it. As a result, every thought and every idea presented must withstand the examination of the history. The whole team can sense the tension from different circles of society and realize how heavy their responsibility is. In the end, all the team members have reached a conclusion that this project should start from the premise of respecting history and make it a fundamental starting point that history speaks for itself. We will act with prudence and good faith in this endeavor.

公司的项目团队在2015年6月下旬得知成功中标后,十分高兴。但此次项目的难度却非同以往,起初甚至有些始料未及。作为第二个国家公祭日相关活动的重要组成部分,展馆要求在12月1日必须开馆,工期严格限制,时间紧,任务重;而实际现场仍然处于建筑修复的状态,不能交付,给展陈的设计和施工都带来了相当大的困难。另外,在设计投标阶段,我们的方案存在过度设计,对于展览主题的把握不够到位等问题,专家小组并不满意,需要在有限的时间内,准确体会与把握展览特性,用艺术的语言准确地表达展陈主旨。困难重重,却绝无后退之理,以勇气之躯与智慧之心,迎难而上,力求交出一份让社会各方都满意的答卷。

在与公司陈国欢总经理充分讨论后,我们一致决定将公司的人力、物力向项目倾斜,最大限度给予支持,保证项目的顺利完成。对内,迅速调集精兵强将,科学统筹,有序组织,成立设计与施工两支队伍,分别由公司设计总监任睿和工程分公司经理陶萍全权负责。在两支队伍内部,根据分工、专业方向再进行科学分组,强化管理,实现项目过程中各工作环节的有序衔接,以应对项目的各种情况,确保项目的有序推进。对外,积极与业主方侵华日军南京大屠杀遇难同胞纪念馆的朱馆长及其内容团队、负责建筑修复工程的南京大学建筑设计院、负责项目代建施工的南京市城建集团项目工程公司沟通对接,派驻人员进驻现场,了解情况,紧密配合,共同推进,确保项目的有序推进。

在布展设计的深化阶段,设计团队全员废寝忘食,阅读文本,解读文物,深入思考,充分讨论,力求准确把握展陈的主旨与内涵,为展陈寻"魂",希望能够打动观众,震撼心灵,唤起观者与展览间的共鸣,让这份血泪历史为人们所铭记。针对"慰安妇"主题,我们曾提出了包括"枯萎的花朵""禁锢的牢笼""挣扎的灵魂""悲怆的泪滴"等多个意象用以串联整体展览,在与时任侵华日军南京大屠杀遇难同胞纪念馆馆长、利济巷慰安所旧址修缮保护和陈列布展工程专家组组长朱成山再三商榷后,最终选定了最能够反映"慰安妇"悲怆状态的"泪滴"作为设计元素。

We were thrilled to learn that our project team won the bid at the end of June, 2015. However, this project has been unprecedentedly difficult; more difficult than we first expected. As an important part of the related activities prepared for the second National Memorial Day, it was required that the exhibition hall must be opened on December 1, so the construction period was very limited and the task was heavy. However, at that time the site was still in repair and could not be handed over, which posed trouble with regards to the design and construction of the exhibitions. Additionally, when we were designing our submission in the bidding process, our scheme was over-designed and we didn't understand the exhibition theme well, so the expert team was not quite satisfied with our scheme. Therefore, we needed to grasp the unique features of this exhibition site and to precisely express the main idea of the exhibition site with artistic language. Though difficulties lay ahead, we couldn't retreat from them. Rather, we embraced them with our courage and wisdom and completed the project to the satisfaction of the whole society. After consulting with the general manager of our company, we made an unanimous decision that human and material resources would be allocated to this project to the utmost extent so as to ensure the completion of the project. Inside our company, competent employees were gathered and organized into two teams, namely the designing team and the construction team. These teams were led by Ren Rui, chief executive of design, and Tao Ping, manager of the engineering department. Inside the two teams, members were subdivided into groups according to their expertise, so that management could be strengthened and every working phase of the project could be linked. This can also ensure quick response to emergency and advance the speed of the project. What's more, we initiated discussion with Mr. Zhu, the curator and proprietor of The Memorial Hall of the Victims in Nanjing Massacre by Japanese Invaders, the team in charge of the exhibition items of the memorial hall, the School of Architectural Design of Nanjing University and the Nanjing Urban Construction Investment Holdings Group. We also stationed people on site to get first-hand information so as to enhance cooperation and advance the project together. During the later stage of designing the exhibitions, all the members of the designing team spared spent time reading the text and studying the relics. They went through deep thinking and heated discussion to ensure an accurate understanding of the theme and the connotation of the exhibitions. They hoped to find the "soul" of the exhibitions, so as to touch the audience, resonate with them and enable them to keep in mind the bitter history of the site. As for the theme of "comfort women", we put forward several images such as "withered flowers", "chained cage", "struggling spirits" and "mournful tears" to connect the exhibitions. After rounds of discussions with Mr. Zhu, the curator of The Memorial Hall of the Victims in Nanjing Massacre by Japanese Invaders and leader of the experts group of Nanjing Museum of Site of Lijixiang Comfort Stations restoration and exhibition planning project, we finally chose "Tears" as the design element, because they are the most reflective symbol of the "comfort women".

展览概况 GENERAL SITUATION OF THE EXHIBITION SITE

在朱成山馆长的创意指导下，室外空间结合环境，从墙面到地面分别设计了"泪洒一面墙""泪湿一片地""泪滴一条路"三大部分，将室外环境有机串联，丰富了展陈内涵。室内展览作为展陈的核心主体，则经历了多次的反复，设计方案一稿一稿地讨论修改，逐步丰富、完善，越来越触动人心。而作为整个展陈的点睛之笔，序厅"无言的泪"以及A区展览尾声"流不尽的泪"则是对主题的又一次升华，以此突出刻画了"慰安妇"受害者们这段血泪历史的痛苦与凄怆。

"千淘万漉虽辛苦，吹尽黄沙始到金。"只有树立自我的高标准、严要求，勇于自我否定，不断突破自我、精益求精，才能真正打造出一个精品项目。四个多月夜以继日的奋战，这其中的万般艰辛都被南京利济巷慰安所旧址陈列馆如期开馆的喜悦与自豪所取代。爱涛人以自己心中无比的热忱，满怀着强烈的责任感与神圣的使命感，团结协作，勇于开拓，敢于担当，攻坚克难，以无比的勇气、真挚的情怀、非凡的智慧，构筑捍卫正义的国家记忆，印刻个体的血泪之殇，承担传播正义与和平的社会之责，为民族、为国家、为社会、为同胞贡献自己的力量。

Under the creative instruction of Mr.Zhu, we combined the outdoor space with the surroundings and designed three major parts from the walls to the ground, which were named "Tears on the Walls", "Tears on the Ground" and "Tears on the Road". The combination with outdoor surroundings enriched the meaning of the exhibition. As a central part of the exhibition, the indoor exhibitions went through revisions many times. The design scheme was revised again and again and was finally improved to a point of perfection that would move people. As the punch line of the whole exhibition, "the silent tears" in the preface hall and "the endless tears" in the end of the Area A reiterated the theme and highlighted the bitter experiences that the "comfort women" have suffered.

"Sweetness comes after overcoming difficulties." Only by establishing high standards and requirements, subjecting oneself to them and exceeding oneself can we build an excellent project. Even though we went through countless difficulties for over four months, we felt thrilled and proud when the Nanjing Museum of Site of Lijixiang Comfort Stations was opened as scheduled. We Artallers, with passion, sense of responsibility and mission, worked together to overcome difficulties. Under the motivation of unparalleled courage, sincere sympathy and great wisdom, we've safeguarded the memory of our nation, preserved the tragic historical records for those victims, and shouldered the social responsibility of carrying on justice and peace. We've made our contribution for our nation, our country and our compatriots.

个人简介

陈思宁

江苏爱涛文化有限公司总经理兼法人代表。早期负责以城市景观为主的环境艺术相关业务。而后凭借自己对市场发展动向的敏锐判断，开始主动进入文博展陈市场，在搭建公司架构、组建专业团队、开拓行业市场等方面均发挥了核心作用，打造了诸如南京博物院、山西省博物院、甘肃省博物馆等一系列国内重点工程。经过十几年的经营与发展，已将爱涛打造成为国内知名的文化品牌和行业内最具影响力的一流公司之一。

Chen Sining, as the general manager and legal representative of Jiangsu Artall Cultural Industry Co. Ltd., was in charge of business related environmental art which is urban landscape oriented in her early working period. By virtue of her keen judgment on the market development trend, she started to set foot in museum exhibition market where she played a central role in organizing the company structure, forming a professional team and expanding the market and built a series of key projects in China such as Nanjing Museum, Shanxi Museum and Gansu Provincial Museum, etc. After decades of management and development, Artall has become one of the most well-known and influential cultural brand as well as a company in exhibition industry.

设计的情感
FEELING OF DESIGN

我一直都认为陈列设计师赋予作品的情感,是与广义室内设计师之间最大的区别。一切围绕展馆主题而成立的空间、形式、展柜、灯光以及数字手段,都不仅仅停留在形式阶段,更多的是蕴含了历史的面貌和设计者的感悟,二次呈现于观众的眼前。美国符号论美学家苏珊·朗格在她的著作《情感与形式》中论述了情感对绘画、雕塑、建筑、音乐、舞蹈等一系列艺术类别的影响。我想,对于陈列艺术这一公共艺术形式,情感同样具有指导意义和借鉴作用。

像利济巷慰安所旧址陈列馆这样的项目,就是给予我和我的团队的一个重大的设计挑战。它既不是传统意义上的博物馆,也非当下热闹纷扰的展示中心。闹市里宁静的遗址建筑,在时代变迁中见证着历史,需要我们去表述业已流逝的光阴,去标记受难者曾经的伤痛,让逝者安息,让生者铭记。所以,我们要在历史与观众间搭设桥梁,使观众能够了解到、感悟到展览的初衷。

As I always believe, the emotion that visual designers put into their work is exactly what distinguish them from interior designers in broad sense. Spaces, forms, showcases, light and digital applications assembled under the theme are far more than form, but have re-rendered the history and the designer's feelings to audience. Susanne K. Langer, an American semiotic aesthetician, once elaborated in her book *Feeling and Form* the influence of feelings on painting, sculpture, architecture, music, dance and a series of other arts. I supposed that this book will also inform exhibit art.

It's a big challenge to me as well as my team to design a project as Nanjing Museum of Site of Lijixiang Comfort Stations. It is neither a conventional museum nor a modern exhibition center. It is a silent relic in the bustling metropolis. We need to present time that has passed away and engrave the painfulness of those sufferers, so as to comfort the dead and alarm the living. Therefore, we are to bridge history and audience, leading our audience to the original intention of this exhibition.

坐落在南京市利济巷的民国建筑群落,具有典型的民国建筑特征,百年未满却也历经沧桑。夕阳下的建筑外貌是她最佳的观赏时间。血色残阳倾洒在斑驳的黄色立面上,建筑之间的投影相互交织,历史的气息在静谧无声中缓缓流动。

Located in Lijixiang, Nanjing, these buildings are featured with Republic of China era, which has witnessed ups and downs even in less than one hundred years. Twilight is the best time to appreciate these buildings. With blood-red sunlight casting on the mottled yellow walls and the shadows of buildings overlapping with each other, the atmosphere of history flows around in silence, and the theme of "comfort women" imposes some gloomy and depression on this silence.

| 展览概况 GENERAL SITUATION OF THE EXHIBITION SITE

而"慰安妇"这一题材，则使静谧中多了凝重与压抑。对于这种类型的项目，我们的方法是首先做加法，设计团队在初期头脑风暴的创意过程中着重于元素的提炼，罗列出一系列适合的形式语言用以设计备选，比如枯萎的花朵、流淌的眼泪、蔓延的毒素、禁锢的灵魂等，不一而足。然后在有了一定的思考与积累后进一步梳理，仔细分析元素所能表现出来的内在含义和外在形象，同文本内容做对接、融合。牵强的、不充分的元素予以摒弃，而统一的、协调的元素暂时保留，直至在形式设计的过程中不断调整和淘汰，去芜存菁。比如：毒素的渗透形式或许适合表现日军慰安所制度向全亚洲扩散这一内容主题，而枯萎的花朵正寓意为女性的受难者，禁锢的灵魂和建筑功能之间又有着一定的联系和想象。最后，则必须忍痛割爱，大刀阔斧地砍去大部分素材，保留核心的、标志性的元素，将主题、形式、内容三者恰如其分地融合而落于一点，以保证主题的整体形象和形式的高度浓缩，从而实现展览内涵的深度表达。

To deal with this kind of project, we first had our design team to have brainstorm, mainly to abstract essential elements and list a string of formal language for design to choose from, eg. withered flowers, running tears, spreading toxin, chained souls, etc. and then we made further combing after thinking and accumulation, giving a close analysis on the underlying meaning and the external image of each elements to match and integrate them with texts. We abandoned those inappropriate elements and maintain those appropriate ones. By continuous adjustments and selections in formal design, we finally weed out the incompatible elements. For example, spreading toxin may well express that the comfort houses were spreading aroud Asia and the withered flowers symbolize women victims. Besides, accociations may exist between chained souls and the function of these buildings. At last, we were only able to maintain core and representative elements and voted out most materials we put forward at first. We appropriately integrated theme, form and contents to one point to establish an integrated theme and a fully abstracted form, so as to give a full expression to the underlying meaning of this exhibition.

用泪滴来覆盖全场，是大家一致认为较为恰当的。哭泣的形象，让观众和受难者之间形成心理上的共鸣。而无论是具象的亦或抽象的表达手段又从"哭泣"本身得以扩充。我的想法是用泪滴的形态来串联文本内容各章节，在视觉传达的领域给予观众引导。但在每个章节核心内容的提升上，则需要立足于泪滴的基础，以更为形象或者说更为高水准的手段来诠释，用以概括内容的内涵，加深观众的记忆和理解。比如，我们在序厅的表现上大胆创意，仔细求证。彻底抛除展馆序厅固有的、约定俗成的思路，不做表面文章，不拘泥于传统的壁画、浮雕等艺术表现形式。把笔触点向观众内心深处，用尖锐的、带刺的铁丝网裹挟着泪滴和"慰安妇"幸存者的照片，缠绕纠葛、支离破碎、盘旋而上，最终形成龙卷风般的造型。挣扎与痛苦、无法逃离的窒息感、战争席卷所带来的创伤、种种意义、情绪全部表达得淋漓尽致，无须再刻意诉说什么。

We all agree that it is well suited to cover the whole exhibition with tears. The image of crying will arise empathy for the victims from the bottom of audience's heart. And the "crying" image is where our methods of expression, tangible or intangible, start. I would like to string up textual sections with tears and guide audience by visual communication. We need to firmly rooted in "tears" when sublimate the core of each section, rendering them with more elaborated techniques to enhance the audience memory and understanding. For example, in the design of preface hall, we resorted to innovative expressions and close investigations, jumping out of inherent and conventional ideas about preface hall and breaking out of the limitation of traditional expression forms like mural and emboss. Instead, we touch the bottom of audience's hearts, wrapping tears and photos of surviving comfort women with sharp and barbed wire which twining, shattering and winding up to assemble a tornado. Without any additional words, the struggling and suffering, the inescapable choking depression and the trauma brought about by the overwhelming war are totally demonstrated.

再比如，在介绍"慰安妇"制度展览的末尾阶段，我们在文本的基础上增设一个互动装置。以受难妇女幸存者的形象塑造了一个雕塑胸像，内藏水循环系统，水滴缓缓从空洞的眼眶中溢出，正如流不尽的眼泪一般，无论观众如何擦拭，眼泪总会在一定程度上湿润着雕塑的脸颊。这就使得观众从枯燥的文字图片中解脱出来，通过更直接的感官体会到内在的核心主旨。

For another example, at the end of exhibition, we introduced an interactive device based on text. We sculptured a bust for a victim woman and put a water cycling system inside, thus water teems steadily out of her empty eyes like tears. No matter how will does the audience sweep for her, the tears will always wet out her face. This device has released audience from tiring texts and proctures to have a more direct sensory understanding about the theme.

方案总设计：任睿
CHIEF DESIGNER: REN RUI

材料和设备的选择上也是如此，并非时下流行的就是最好的，也并非最贵的就是最恰当的。我们都同意在陈列设计中，材料和设备是主题创意后的延伸，二者不是割裂的步骤，而是紧密联系的。为了在洁净空间中控制观众的视线范围，我们甚至越俎代庖，主动与建筑、暖通、照明、安防等多方协调，使这些杂乱无章的点位集中、有序地合成在规定的架构之中。为了让图文更具历史的沧桑感，我们用油画布作为展板的载体，油墨在布面上所呈现出立体而又强烈的肌理品质，将丰富而饱满的情绪倾泄而出。这样的细节还有许多，更多地考验了团队的创意能力和领衔者的控制能力。

一次设计旅程，就是一次精神洗礼。陈列设计的魅力即在于此。如电影般，大纲就是剧本，设计师就像是导演、摄影、剪辑、美术、后期，甚至还兼职演员，只有全然沉浸其中，用心体会与感悟，才能完成角色赋予的使命。你先与尘封旧事沟通，再同后来者娓娓道来。所以你不仅是美术的设计者，更是历史的艺术家。

设计过程的一点感悟，与诸君共勉。

We followed the same principle in material and equipment selection. We neither follow the most popular ones nor the most expensive ones. We had an agreement that in exhibit design, materials and equipments are extentions of theme innovation, which are rather closely connected than separated. To control the visual field of audience in clear space, we even went beyond our responsibility to actively cooperate with people responsible for construction, heating, lightening and safety securities to integrate these discrete parts into a regulated framework. To give the texts and pictures a sense of history, we covered our display board with canvas. Emotion torrent out from this spatial and intense texture of printing ink on canvas. Details like this can be seen everywhere, which demonstrates the innovation of a team and the control ability of a team leader.

Every designing can be a spiritual cleansing, which underlies the charm of exhibit design. Exhibit design is like filmmaking, which outline is script, designer is director, cameramen, film cutters, art designers, post producers and even part-time actors. Only when you put all your heart into it, feeling and percepting with heart, can you give a full play to your role. You need to communicate with history and then tell latecomers the story. Therefore, you are not only a artistic designer, but also a historical artist.

I would be really delighted if my shallow understandings in design would be somehow informed.

个人简介

任睿
江苏江阴人，
出生于1976年。
由于专业及爱好，1999年自无锡轻工大学设计学院毕业至今，一直致力于文博展陈工作。数十年来，多次领衔设计大型博物馆室内陈列。
主要作品有：甘肃省博物馆、陕西历史博物馆、南京博物院等重点项目的陈列设计。

Ren Rui is from Jiangyin of Jiangsu Province and was born in 1976.
Because of his major and interest, he has been devoting himself to museum exhibition work since he graduated from Design School of Wuxi Light Industry University. For the past ten years or more, he has been the chief designer for many major museum exhibitions.
His major works include the exhibition designs for Gansu Museum, Shaanxi History Museum and Nanjing Museum.

设 计
团 队
DESIGNING TEAM

| 设计团队　DESIGNING TEAM |

岑静
空间设计师
Ceng Jing
Space Designer

周紫金
布展设计师
Zhou Zijin
Exhibition Designer

江燕
视觉传达设计师
Jiang Yan
Visual Designer

张弛
空间设计师
Zhang Chi
Space Designer

蒋新平
布展设计师
Jiang Xinping
Exhibition Designer

陶晓杰
文案策划
Tao Xiaojie
Text Writing Designer

高伦
空间设计师
Gao Lun
Space Designer

任睿
方案总设计
Ren Rui
Chief Designer

陆建
主案设计师
Lu Jian
Designing Manager

▶ | 核心设计团队介绍　INTRODUCTION OF CORE DESIGN TEAM |

　　设计团队在行业资深设计师任睿担纲领衔下，由一批行业内极具实力与潜力的设计师和策划人员组成，涉及空间设计、视觉传达设计、布展设计以及策划四种细分专业人才，可应对各种行业需求。经过多年洗礼，团队具备了过硬的专业实力，积累了丰富的实战经验，能够胜任各类博物馆的展览设计、策划工作。

Under the leadership of Ren Rui, a senior designer in designing industry, the designing team consists of a group of designers and planners who have great strength and potentials in the field, which involves four kinds of professional talents to meet various requirements in space design, visual communication design, exhibition design and planning. After focusing on designing for many years, now it has excellent professional strength and a wealth of practical experiences, which makes it competent for all kinds of museum exhibition designing and planning.

室外展陈
OUTDOOR EXHIBITION

室外展陈

　　空间环境是展陈的重要组成部分，作为遗址展览馆，建筑遗址本身即是重要的展品之一，更是曾经那段血泪历史的见证与重要承载。而以能够反映"慰安妇"悲怆状态的"泪滴"作为意象，通过多角度的表达，串起室外展览，使其与室内的主体展览相呼应，并从新角度定义了"遗址"展览。

Outdoor surroundings is an important part of the exhibition. As site exhibition hall, the old buildings themselves are part of the exhibitions and act as witness and carrier for the historical tragedy. "Tears" as image are used to reflect the sadness of "comfort women". Through different means of expression, the outdoor exhibition is connected with main exhibition inside to make them correspond with each other, giving a new perspective to this "site" exhibition.

室外展陈　OUTDOOR EXHIBITION

利济巷慰安所旧址陈列馆全景图

"慰安妇"主题雕塑位于展馆主入口处,由著名雕塑家吴显林创作,以"二战"时随军记者拍摄的中国战场上怀孕的朝鲜籍"慰安妇"朴永心的照片为创作原型。

雕塑由三位"慰安妇"组成,其中身怀六甲的"慰安妇"为主要人物,她身形虚弱,一手护住腹中胎儿,一手搭在另一妇女背上,显得无力、无助与无望。

Text for the main sculpture: "comfort-women"-themed sculpture is situated at the main entrance of the exhibition hall. It was created by well-known sculptor Wu Xianlin, based on the photo of Pak Young Sim, a pregnant Korean "comfort woman" in China. Her photo was taken by a military journalist of the Second World War. The sculpture is composed with three "comfort women", of whom the pregnant "comfort woman" is the central character. She is feeble and has one hand put on her belly to protect the fetus and another hand put on another woman for support, which shows how powerless, helpless and desperate she is.

慰安妇形象主题雕塑

室外展陈 OUTDOOR EXHIBITION

"泪洒一面墙"

水晶泪

▶ 泪洒一面墙设计稿

在陈列馆的外墙上，挂着十几颗由铂晶制成的巨大"泪滴"，寓意着"泪洒一面墙"，斑驳陈旧的墙面上，仿佛可见硕大的泪滴，折射出她们的无助与绝望。

On the exterior wall of the exhibition hall hang a dozens of giant poukim "tears", which expresses the meaning of "tears on the wall". It seems that big tears can be seen from the mottled old wall, reflecting their helplessness and desperation.

室外展陈 OUTDOOR EXHIBITION

22

一面巨大的黑白照片墙上,是"慰安妇"一张张饱经岁月风霜的面孔,有的人在仰天呐喊,有的人在低头抹泪。照片墙下方,是一块湿漉漉的土地。时间的年轮虽已过去半个多世纪,"慰安妇"幸存者们饱经岁月风霜的面孔上泪水流淌着,浸湿了地面。这是对日军实施"慰安妇"制度无言的控诉。

On a big wall hang a lot of black and white photos of aging faces of the long-suffering "comfort women". Some are crying to heaven for help and some are wiping their tears with heads down. Below the photo wall is a piece of moist land. Though half of century has passes by, tears of the "comfort women" survivors trickle down and wet the ground, which demonstrates a silent denouncement against the Japanese military "comfort women" system.

| 泪湿一片地设计稿 |

| 室外展陈 OUTDOOR EXHIBITION |

窖井盖上是一滴滴眼泪形状,寓意着"慰安妇"们痛苦的泪水,曾经吧嗒吧嗒地滴落在慰安所内每一条路上。

Tears were carved on the manhole covers, indicating that the bitter tears of "comfort women" used to fall down on every road of the "comfort houses".

"泪滴一条路"

室内展陈
INDOOR EXHIBITION

室内展览由"基本陈列""旧址陈列""专题陈列"以概转论,铺承开来。"基本陈列"空间相对开阔、贯通,展览纯粹,特以内容、实物为本,并辅以日军"慰安妇"幸存者采访视频佐证。通过序厅"无言的泪"渲染,楼梯转角"歌剧秋子"再现,二楼"自然光"处理,尾厅"流不尽的泪"升华,以使展览深入人心。"旧址陈列"以"间"为单元,保持原建筑格局,特以门厅、日军"慰安妇"幸存者朴永心指认的19号房间、盥洗间复原,呈现原"日军东云慰安所"景况,主展南京部分日军慰安所以及日军"慰安妇"幸存者相关内容,警醒世人,铭记历史。"专题陈列"以线贯穿,曲折蜿蜒,空间错综复杂,内容涉及上海、全国各地、朝鲜半岛、东南亚、太平洋诸岛乃至日本本土,以展现日军"慰安妇"制度的扩散,全面反思日军无道德、反人类行径,警示世界,珍视和平。

Indoor exhibition was arranged from general to specific, including "Basic Exhibition", "Site Exhibition" and "Theme Exhibition". "Basic Exhibition" occupies a space which is relatively spacious and cut-through. The exhibition is simplified, centered on texts and items and added by the interview videos of the surviving "comfort women" as proof. Walking through the preface hall "Silent Tears", "Opera Akiko" at the corner of stairway, "Natural Light" on the second floor and "Endless Tears" at the end of the hall, viewers will be deeply moved by the exhibition. "Site Exhibition" identifies "one single room" as a unit and keeps the original layout. The hallway, room No.19 which was identified by the surviving "comfort woman" Pak Young Sim and the bathroom were restored to what "Japanese Dongyun Comfort House" used to look like. This part exhibits some of Japanese "comfort houses" in Nanjing and relevant contents donated by "comfort women" survivors to warn the living not to forget history. "Theme Exhibition" is more complicated but has a thread running through it. Its contents are related to "comfort women" ranging from Shanghai, other places of China, Korean peninsula, Southeast Asia and various islands on Pacific Ocean to even Japan itself, which shows how serious it was that Japanese Military "Comfort Women" System spread over a vast territory and what kind of immoral and anti-human crimes that Japanese troops have committed. They serve to warn people around the world and makes us cherish peace.

▶ A区基本陈列 BASIC EXHIBITION IN AREA A

B区旧址陈列　SITE EXHIBITION IN AREA B

C区专题陈列　THEME EXHIBITION IN AREA C

| A区基本陈列　BASIC EXHIBITION IN AREA A |

　　基本陈列详细地介绍了"慰安妇"制度的始末，为全展之统领。以时间为序，通过翔实的文字、丰富的史料图片以及大量的文物，将"慰安妇"制度的起源、确立、实施、扩大及战后世界各方对于慰安妇制度的态度及认识进行了全面、详细的展览。通过序厅"无言的泪"及尾声"流不尽的泪"两大展项突出了展陈主题，点明了展陈之魂。

Basic Exhibition explains in detail the whole story of "comfort women" system, which serves as general introduction of this exhibition. Based on the time line, the detailed texts, abundant historical records and photos , and a lot of relics not only illustrate the origins, the establishment, the enforcement and expanding of the"comfort women"system, but also state the attitude and understanding of the "comfort women" system. The two major exhibitions --the preface hall "silent tears" and the end hall "endless tears"--emphasize the theme of this exhibition and point out the soul of it.

| 室内展陈　INDOOR EXHIBITION |

序厅空间效果

序厅空间效果

室内展陈　INDOOR EXHIBITION

序厅艺术装置

室内展陈　INDOOR EXHIBITION

序厅前言墙

前　　言

"慰安妇"是指被迫为日本军人提供性服务、充当性奴隶的妇女。战时，日本军国主义以欺骗、掳掠、强迫等手段，为远离本土、数量庞大的日本军队配备了从中国，朝鲜半岛，菲律宾、印度尼西亚、泰国、缅甸、越南等东南亚各地及太平洋诸岛、日本本土等地强征了大量的年轻女子充当性奴隶，建立了完备的军队"慰安妇"制度。中国是日军"慰安妇"制度最大的受害国，日军在中国设立的慰安所最多、时间最长、规模最大，先后有20多万女性被强制沦为日军的性奴隶，相当数量的女性在日军残暴的性虐待中死去。日本军国主义实施的"慰安妇"制度是践踏妇女人权、违反国际人道法规、违反战争常规并制度化了的国家犯罪行为，是法西斯对女性的集体奴役，突出体现了日本军国主义的野蛮、残忍和暴虐，也是战争带给人类的最惨痛、最刻骨铭心的记忆。

PREFACE

"Comfort Woman" is a general term for women affiliated with sexual slavery by Japanese troops, most of whom were sex slaves recruited forcibly by Japanese army. During World War II, the Japanese Militarism recruited a large quantity of young women from Austronesia, Japan and other Southeast Asian countries including China, Korean Peninsula, Philippines, Indonesia, Thailand, Burma and Vietnam, serving as sex slaves for considerable Japanese soldiers far away from home through cheating, kidnapping and compelling. A thorough military "Comfort Women" system was thereby established, from which China suffered most. Japanese army has established "Comfort Stations" in China longest in time, and largest in quantity and scale. More than 200 thousand women successively forced to be sex slaves for Japanese soldiers and a significant number of women died from the Japanese brutal sexual abuse. The "Comfort Women" system has trampled on the human rights of women; violated the international humanitarian law and martial conventions. It is an institutionalized state crime that shows extraordinary savage cruelty and oppression of the Japanese militarism. It is a fascist collective servitude of women and the most painful and unforgettable memory brought by war.

前書き

「慰安婦」とは、強制的に日本軍に性的サービスを提供させられ、性奴隷にされた女性のことを示します。戦時、日本軍国主義は詐欺、略取や強迫等の手段で、日本本土から遠く離れた数量彩大の日本軍のために、中国、朝鮮半島、フィリピン、インドネシア、タイ、ミャンマー、ベトナム等東南アジア各地及び太平洋諸島、また日本本土から大量の若い女性を性奴隷として強制徴集し、完全な軍隊「慰安婦」制度を設立した。中国は日本軍「慰安婦」制度の最大被害国であり、中国で設置された慰安所が最も多く、時間が最も長く、規模が最も大きかったです。20 数万の女性が強制的に日本軍の性奴隷にさせられ、数多くの女性が残酷な性的虐待で命を失いました。日本軍国主義が実施した「慰安婦」制度は、女性の人権を踏みにじ、国際人道法や戦争法規に違反し制度化された国の犯罪行為であり、ファシズムが女性を集団的奴隷化する暴行です。それは、日本軍国主義の野蛮、残酷や暴虐を十分に暴露し、戦争が人類に残した最も悲惨で忘れられない記憶です。

서언

'위안부'란 일본군의 성적 욕구를 해소하기 위하여 성노예가 될 것을 강요당했던 여성을 말한다. 제2차 세계대전 당시 일본군국주의는 기만, 약탈, 강제 등 방법으로 중국과 조선반도, 그리고 필리핀, 인도네시아, 태국, 미얀마, 베트남 등 동남아 각지와 태평양제도, 일본 본토 등지에서 대량의 젊은 여성을 강제 징용하여 일본 본토에서 멀리 떠나 방대한 일본군의 성노예로 삼았으며 완벽한 군대 '위안부'제도를 세웠다. 중국은 일본군 '위안부'제도의 최대 피해국이다. 일본군이 중국에 설치한 위안소는 그 수량이 가장 많고 시간이 가장 길며 규모가 가장 크다. 또한 선후로 20여만 명의 여성이 강제로 일본군의 성노예로 전락하였으며 그중 상당수가 일본군의 잔혹한 성적 학대로 목숨을 잃었다. 일본군국주의가 실시한 '위안부'제도는 여성 인권을 유린하고 국제인도주의 법규를 위반하였으며 전쟁 관례를 위반하고 국가의 범죄행위를 제도화하였으니, 이러한 '위안부'제도는 여성에 대한 파시스트의 집단적 노예화로서 일본군국주의의 만행과 잔인함, 포학함을 적나라하게 구현했을 뿐만 아니라 전쟁이 인류에게 가져다준 가장 쓰라리고 뼈에 사무치는 기억으로 된다.

图文展示

冈村宁次与日本"慰安妇"团
Okamura Yasuji and "Comfort Women" Corps

冈村宁次と日本「慰安婦」団　오카무라 야스지와 일본군 '위안부' 단

1932年1月28日，日军进攻上海，"一·二八"事变爆发。1932年3月，在沪日军已达3万多人。为防止因大规模的强奸事件导致的军纪败坏和性病泛滥，日本上海派遣军副参谋长冈村宁次决定仿照在沪日本海军的做法，从日本关西征调了妇女，组成第一个陆军"慰安妇"团，在吴淞、宝山、庙行和真如等战斗前线为日军官兵提供性服务。

It was on January 28, 1932 when the Japanese army attacked Shanghai, that the January 28 Incident (First Shanghai Incident) broke out. By March, over 30 thousand Japanese soldiers trooped into Shanghai. In order to prevent corruption of disciplines and the proliferation of sexually transmitted diseases caused by large-scale rape incidents, Okamura Yasuji, the Deputy Chief of Staff of Shanghai Expeditionary Army, decided to model the practice of Japanese Marines in Shanghai, recruiting Japanese women from Kansai and organizing the first army "Comfort Women" corps to provide sex service for soldiers in front lines in Wusong, Baoshan, Miaohang, and Zhenru, etc.

"一·二八"事变中，上海闸北宝山区被日军轰炸成一片废墟。
——《中国抗日战争图志》

Zhabei, Baoshan District, Shanghai were bombed into a pile of rubble in the January 28 Incident.
——Pictorial Records of China's War of Resistance against Japan

日本上海派遣军高级参谋冈部直三郎在1932年3月14日的日记中说：近来，士兵四处搜寻妇女的不利情报甚多。此为军队在平时状态下实难避免之事，莫不如积极设立设施，予以认可。多方考虑各种解决士兵性问题之策略，决定着手实施。主要由永见（俊德）中佐承办。

Okabe Naosaburo, Senior Staff of Japan's troops in Shanghai, said in his diary on March 14, 1932: "Recently we have encountered lots of unfavorable information that soldiers are searching for women everywhere. Since it is inevitable in the army in normal state, it's a better choice to accept it and set up some facilitates. In consideration of soldier's sexual desire, I decide to implement the plan and arrange for Chuusa Nagami Shiontoku to undertake it."

冈村宁次1932年3月6日到达上海，7月15日调任关东军副参谋长。1949年2月，冈村宁次在接受记者采访时曾承认："我是无耻至极的'慰安妇'制度的始作俑者"。

Okamura Yasuji arrived in Shanghai on March 6, 1932 and was transferred to Deputy Chief of Staff of the Kwantung Army. He once admitted in an interview in February 1949: "I am an ignoble initiator of the 'Comfort Woman' system."

吴淞、宝山、庙行和真如一线曾是"一·二八"事变的主战场之一，最初的"慰安妇"团就在这里为日本陆军部队提供性服务。
——廖大伟、陈金龙：《侵华日军的自白》

The front line in Wusong, Baoshan, Miaohang and Zhenru was one of the main battlefields of the January 28 Incident where the "Comfort Women" corps originally provided sex service for the army.
——Confessions of Japanese War Criminals edited by Liao Dawei, Chen Jinlong

| 900mm | 900mm | 900mm |

▶ 展墙图版设计稿

室内展陈　INDOOR EXHIBITION

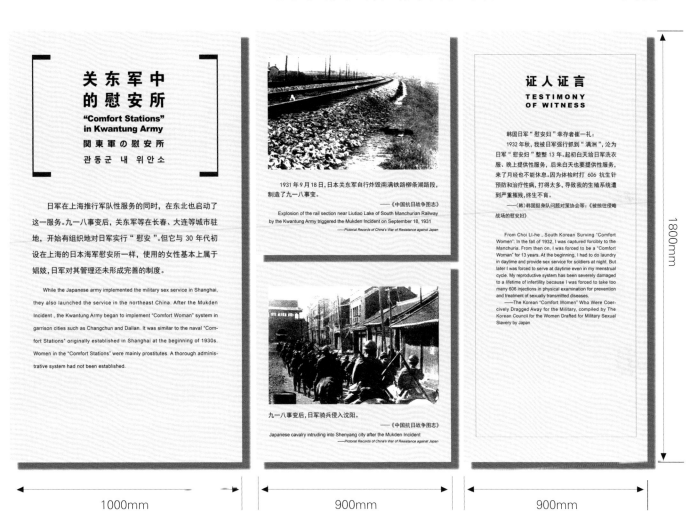

展墙图版设计稿

顶部吊架设计

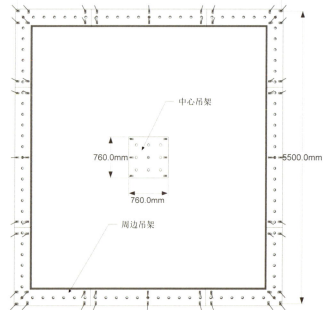

顶部多功能吊架设计稿

室内展陈　INDOOR EXHIBITION

A区顶部多功能吊架设计 THE DESIGN OF MULTI-FUNCTION HANGER FRAME ON THE CEILING OF AREA A

为营造协调的展览空间环境，A区顶部设计多功能吊架。该吊架是集感烟探测器、细水雾喷头、消防广播、监控探头、普通照明、应急照明、轨道射灯为一体的多功能成品吊架。吊架的标准为5500mm×5100mm（部分吊架因空间变化而有局部变化），由中心连接件、四个拐角连接件、四边连接件9个单元组成。吊架由50mm厚的N形框架与顶部链接，下部卡扣为200mm×200mm×100mm标准规格模块。模块包括：射灯模块、筒灯模块、细水雾模块、感烟探测器模块、感温报警器模块、消防广播模块、监控探头模块等7种类型。

A multi-function hanger frame was designed to create a harmonious exhibition environment. The hanger frame consists of smoke detector, water mist fire extinguishing system, fire alarming radio, monitoring probe, common lighting, emergency lighting and track light, all-in-one multi-function finished hanger frame. The standard size for hanger frame is 5500mm× 5100mm (some hanger frames are varied according to the change of space). It is composed of a central connecting device, four corner connecting devices and four edge devices. The hanger frame is connected with the ceiling by an N-shaped frame, whose thickness is 50mm. Its lower buckle is a module with standard size of 200mm×200mm×100mm. The modules include track light module, down light module, water mist module, smoke detector module, temperature-sensing alarming module, fire alarming radio module and monitoring probe module.

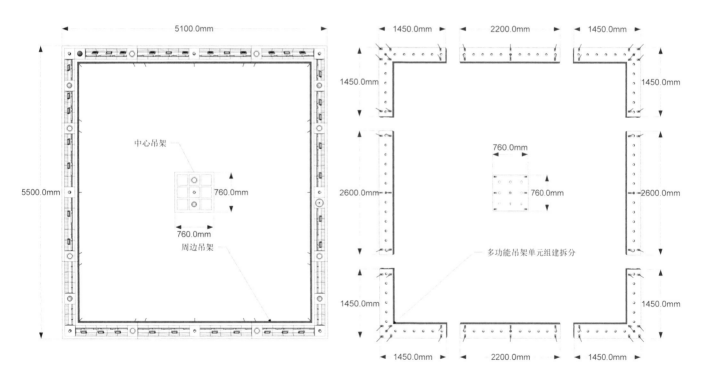

顶部多功能吊架设计稿

室内展陈　INDOOR EXHIBITION

展厅空间

A区顶部多功能吊架设计　THE DESIGN OF MULTI-FUNCTION HANGER FRAME ON THE CEILING OF AREA A

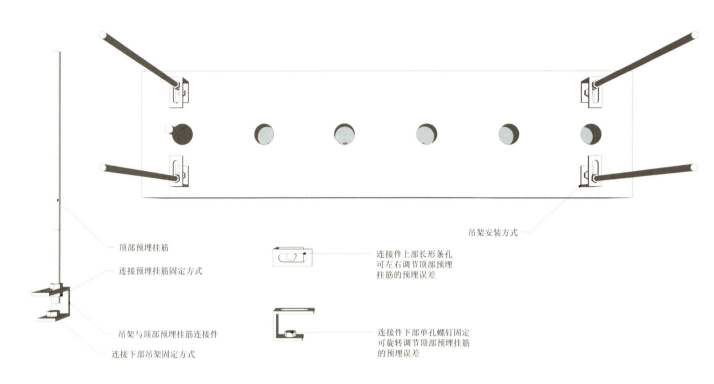

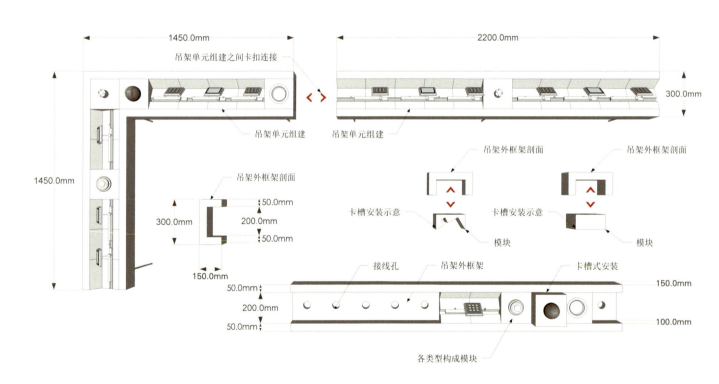

顶部多功能吊架设计稿

室内展陈　INDOOR EXHIBITION

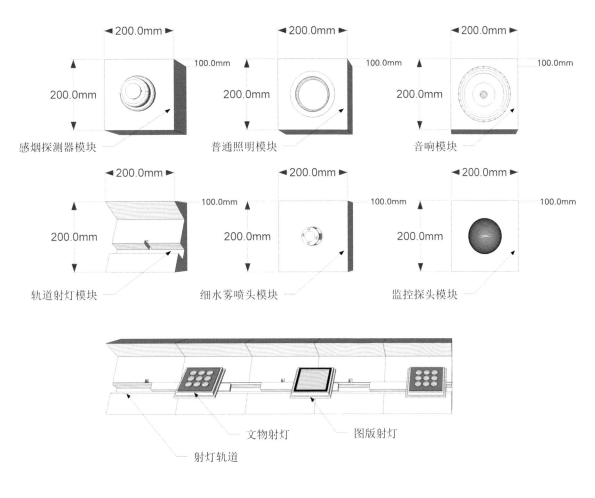
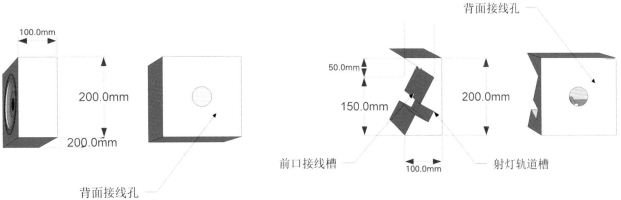

顶部多功能吊架设计稿

室内展陈 INDOOR EXHIBITION

展厅空间

展厅独立展柜设计　THE DESIGN OF THE EXHIBITION CABINETS

独立展柜用以保存展示文物设备，在本次的展览中主要用于展示重点文物。A、B、C区的独立展柜为专门定制，造型统一、干净，边角精细，材料一致。面材为碳烤木，寓意着浴火重生。在尺寸上，考虑空间大小的限制，定制 500mm×500mm、700mm×700mm 两种尺寸。展柜可根据文物保护的不同要求，在下部中空结构中隐藏恒湿机，并用百叶结构遮挡，保证实用性与美观性的统一。

The exhibition cabinets are for preserving the exhibited relics and are used to exhibit key relics in this exhibition. The exhibition cabinets in Area A, B and C are specially made and they look identical in type, clean and have delicate edges. They're made of the same charcoal wood, which means rebirth from the fire. As for their size, due to limited space, they have two sizes, namely 500mm×500mma and 700mm×700mm. According to the different preservation standards of the relics, the constant temperature and humidity machines can be placed in the lower hollow part of the exhibition cabinets and can be hidden by venetian blind to ensure the harmony of their usefulness and aesthetics.

展厅独立展柜设计稿

室内展陈　INDOOR EXHIBITION

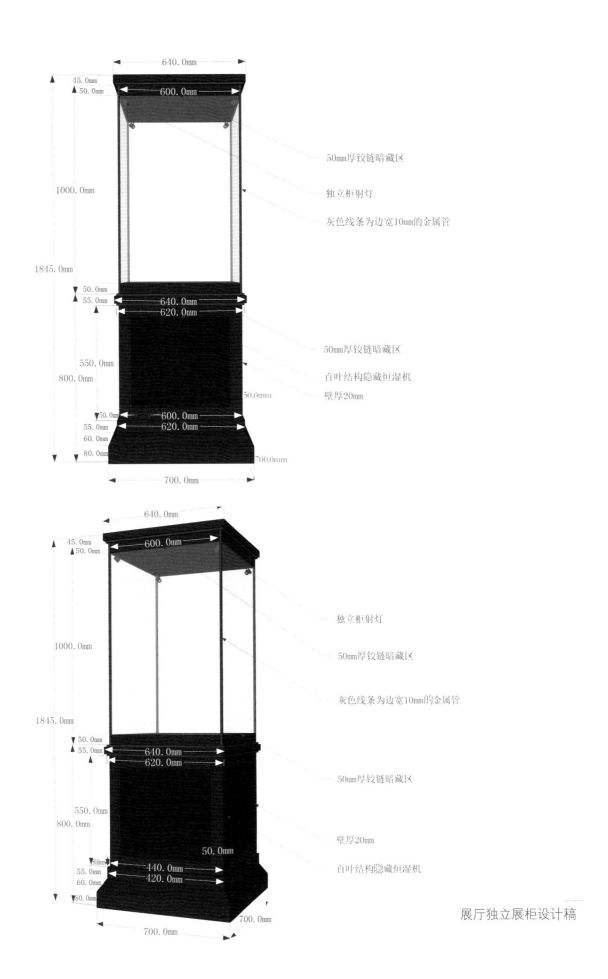

展厅独立展柜设计稿

室内展陈 INDOOR EXHIBITION

展厅空间

| A区独立展墙设计　THE DESIGN OF AN INDEPENDENT EXHIBITION WALL OF AREA A |

为保持展览环境的统一性，在A区设计独立展墙，以隐藏包括明装空调、消防设备在内的基本硬件配套设施。墙体模块尺寸为：1500mm×2800mm×500mm，厚度100mm。

To keep the uniformity of the exhibition environment, an independent exhibition wall was created to conceal some basic equipment such as air conditioners and fire extinguishing equipment. The size of the module wall is 1500mm×2800mm×500mm and its thickness is 100mm.

| 室内展陈　INDOOR EXHIBITION |

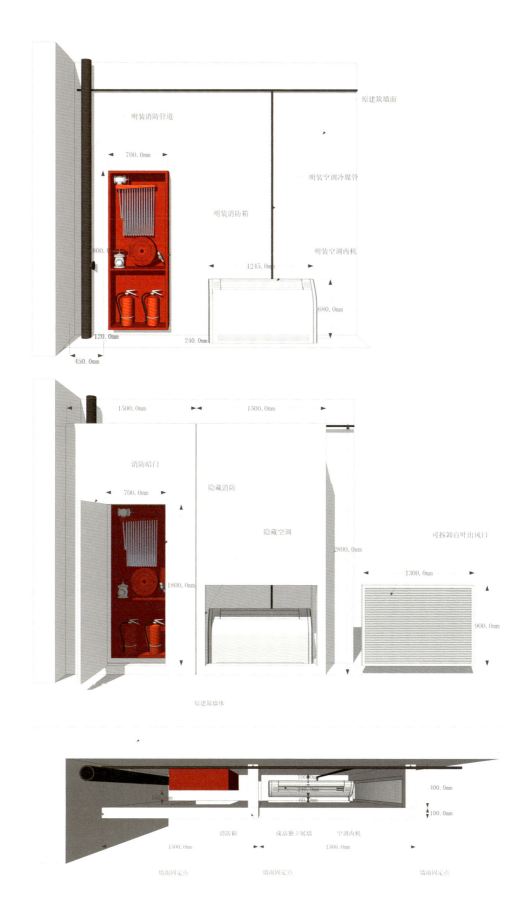

A区独立展墙设计稿

A区独立展墙设计稿

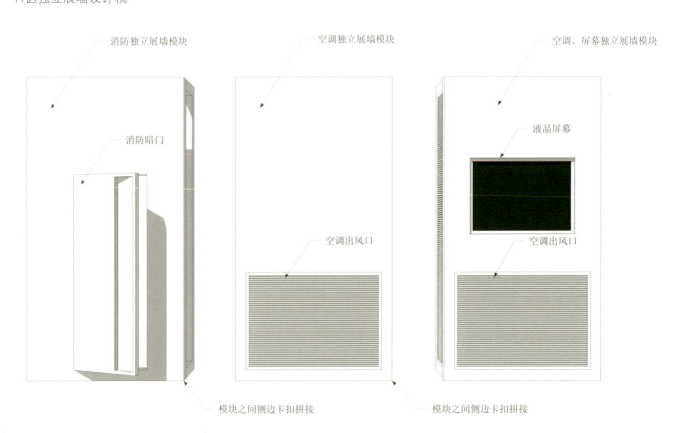

室内展陈　INDOOR EXHIBITION

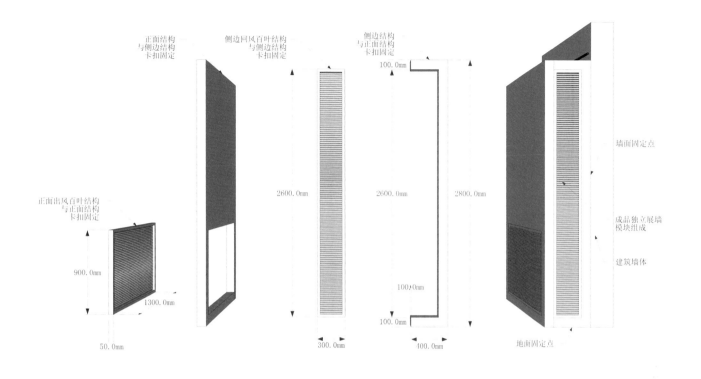
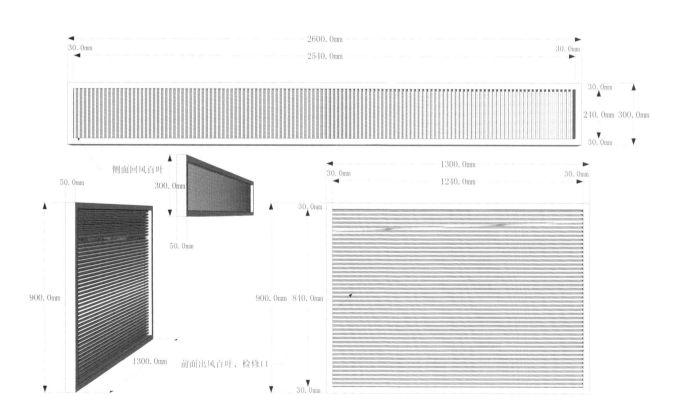

A区独立展墙设计稿

日本籍"慰安妇"
秋子历史场景复原

秋子歌剧片段节选展示方案

顶部灯箱设计方案

室内展陈　INDOOR EXHIBITION

顶部灯箱设计方案

室内展陈　INDOOR EXHIBITION

自然光设计

| 室内展陈 INDOOR EXHIBITION |

▶ | 展厅组合平柜设计　THE DESIGN OF COMBINATION DESK IN THE EXHIBITION HALL |

　　组合平柜用以保存展示文物设备，为本次展览所使用最多的展柜类型。A、B、C区的组合平柜为专门定制，造型统一、干净，边角精细，材料与独立展柜相同。在尺寸上，考虑空间大小的限制，定制600mm×600mm、600mm×1200mm两种尺寸。展柜可根据文物保护的不同要求，在下部中空结构中隐藏恒湿机，并用百叶结构遮挡，保证实用性与美观性的统一。

The combination desk is for preserving the exhibited relics and it has become the most commonly used desk type. The combination desks in Area A, B and C are specially made and they look identical in type, clean and have delicate edges. They're made of the same materials as the independent exhibition cabinet. As for their size, due to limited space, they have two sizes, namely 600mm×600mm and 600mm×1200mm.According to the different preservation standards of the relics,the constant temperature and humidity machines can be placed in the lower hollow part of the exhibition cabinets and can be hidden by venetian blind to ensure the harmony of their usefulness and aesthetics.

| 室内展陈　INDOOR EXHIBITION |

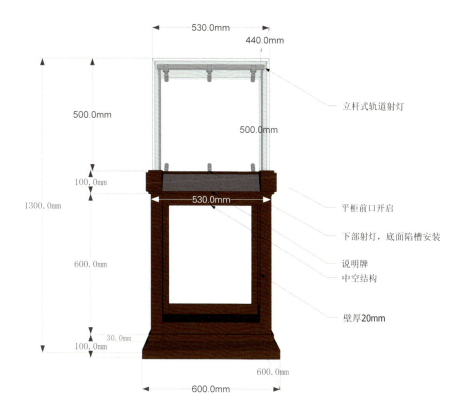
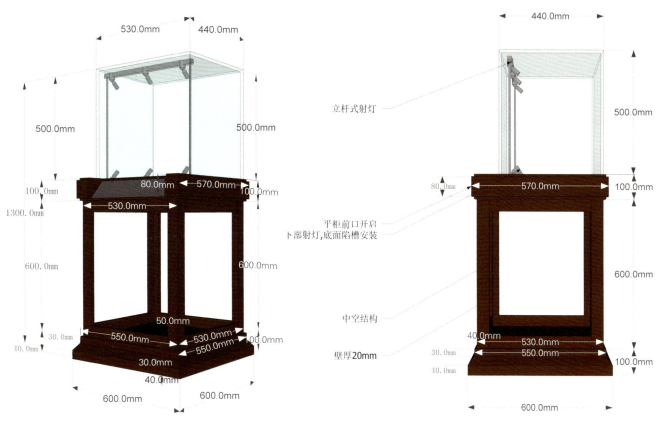

展厅组合平柜设计稿

65

"慰安妇"幸存者周粉英遗留物展示

室内展陈　INDOOR EXHIBITION

2003年11月21日,朝鲜籍日军"慰安妇"幸存者朴永心来到南京利济巷2号慰安所旧址前,回忆自己曾经在此沦为日军性奴隶的三年悲惨经历,禁不住失声痛哭。

On November 21, 2003, Bak Yeong-sim, a surviving "Comfort Woman" from North Korea, burst into tears when she returned to the former site of the "Comfort Station" (now at No.2 Liji Lane) in Nanjing where she had been suffering from inhuman misery for three years.

"慰安妇"幸存者周粉英遗留物展示

展厅组合平柜设计稿

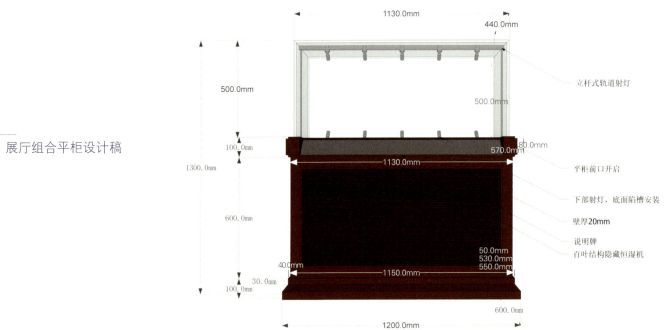

室内展陈　INDOOR EXHIBITION

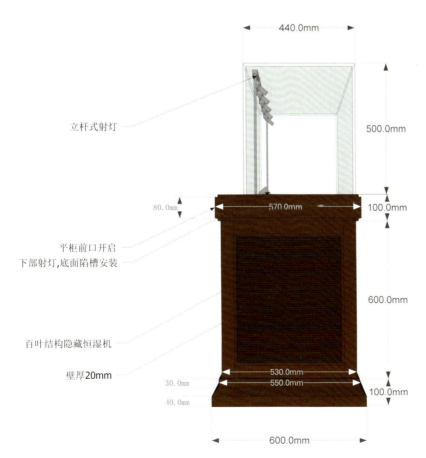

立杆式射灯

平柜前口开启
下部射灯,底面陷槽安装

百叶结构隐藏恒湿机

壁厚20mm

展厅组合平柜设计稿

69

文物展示

室内展陈　INDOOR EXHIBITION

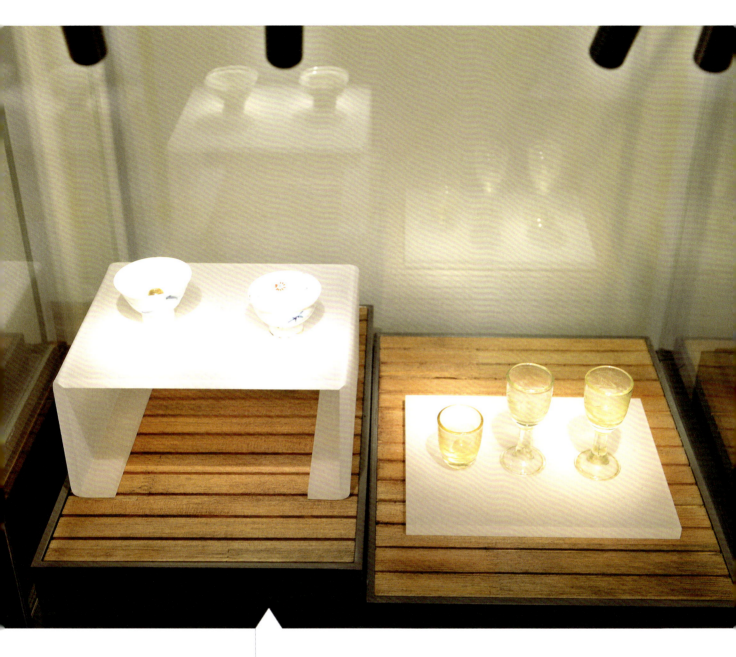

文物展示

文物展示

室内展陈　INDOOR EXHIBITION

重点文物——"慰安妇"照片展示

73

室内展陈 INDOOR EXHIBITION

手提包
——云南省龙陵县董家沟慰安所内"慰安妇"的遗留物,三级文物。
Handbag
——Remains Belonging to "Comfort Women" at Dongjiagou "Comfort Station" in Longling County of Yunnan Province, Class C Cultural Heritage

文物展示

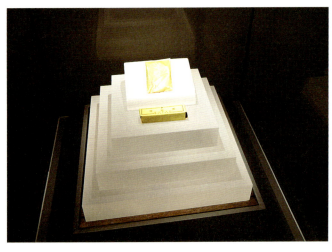
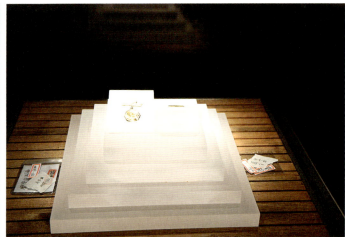

文物展示

室内展陈　INDOOR EXHIBITION

白蒲镇史家巷 1 号中兴旅馆慰安所旧址，系周粉英当年作为"慰安妇"惨遭日军蹂躏的地方。

The former site of Zhongxing Hotel "Comfort Station" at No.1 Shijia Alley, Baipu Town, where Zhou Fenying was raped by the Japanese soldiers.

2007 年 5 月 11 日，侵华日军南京大屠杀遇难同胞纪念馆馆长朱成山一行前往如皋采访并慰问周粉英老人。
——侵华日军南京大屠杀遇难同胞纪念馆藏片

On May 11, 2007, Zhu Chengshan, the curator of Memorial Hall of the Victims in Nanjing Massacre by Japanese Invaders, and his colleagues paid a visit to Zhou Fenying and expressed their deep condolence to her in Rugao.
——Photo collected in the Memorial Hall of the Victims in Nanjing Massacre by Japanese Invaders

| 文物与图版结合展示

"慰安妇"幸存者形象墙

室内展陈　INDOOR EXHIBITION

78

| "流不尽的泪"互动装置设计　THE DESIGN OF THE "ENDLESS TEARS" EQUIPMENT |

　　"流不尽的泪"主题互动装置位于基本陈列展览的尾声，该装置以"慰安妇"林石姑形象的胸像为基础，内藏水循环系统，水滴可缓缓从眼眶中溢出，湿润雕塑的脸颊。观众可亲自擦拭，通过体验进一步感受"慰安妇"那沉重的伤痛，正如那擦不干、流不尽的泪水一般。

The "Endless Tears" equipment was placed at the end of the Basic Exhibition. The equipment is based on a bust of "comfort women" Lin Shigu and has a water circulation system to allow water flow out of the eyes of the bust and wet its face. Viewers can help wipe the tears in person, thus sensing the pain of "comfort women". Their pain is just like the endless tears which can never be wiped out.

B区旧址陈列 SITE EXHIBITION IN AREA B

旧址陈列以日军慰安所"东云楼"旧址建筑为基础，是展陈的核心。其二楼19号房间则为朝鲜籍"慰安妇"朴永心现场指认，意义重大。因此，此区陈列以展现旧址风貌和介绍与南京相关的慰安所及"慰安妇"内容为主。

The site exhibition is based on the old building of Japanese "Dongyunlou Comfort House", which is the center of this exhibition. No.19 room on the second floor has been identified by Korean "comfort woman" Pak Young Sim. That's why it bears extreme significance. Therefore, this part is centered on exhibiting the site and introducing "comfort houses" and "comfort women" related to Nanjing.

室内展陈 INDOOR EXHIBITION

室内展陈　INDOOR EXHIBITION

利济巷慰安所
门厅场景复原

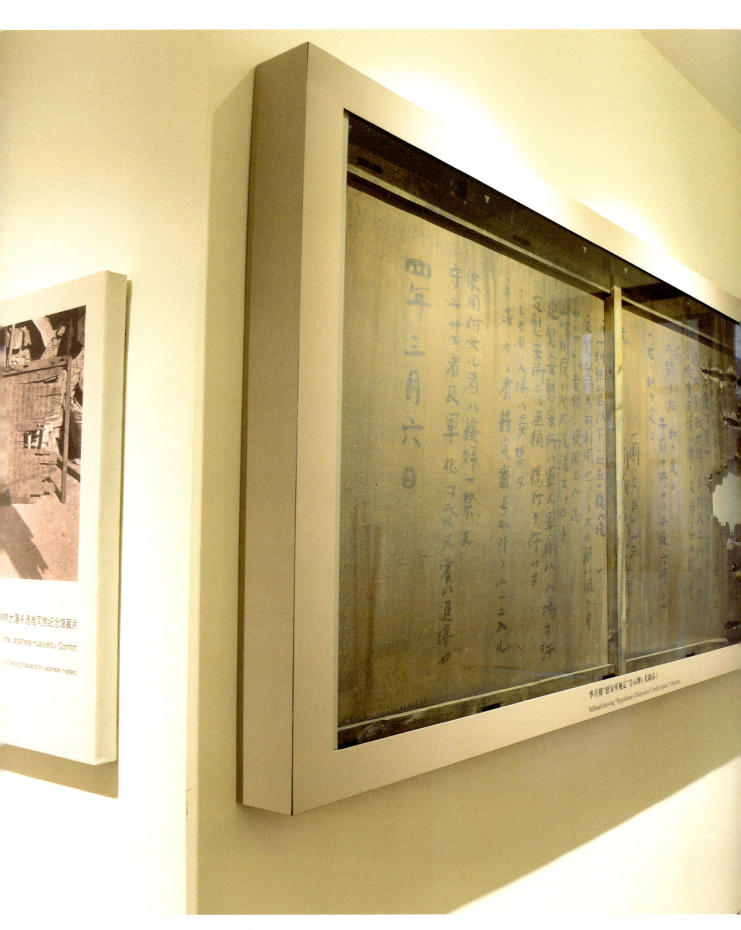

室内展陈　INDOOR EXHIBITION

华月楼慰安所规定
告示牌复原展示

福安里慰安所遗留家具场景复原

室内展陈　INDOOR EXHIBITION

展厅空间

室内展陈　INDOOR EXHIBITION

图文展示

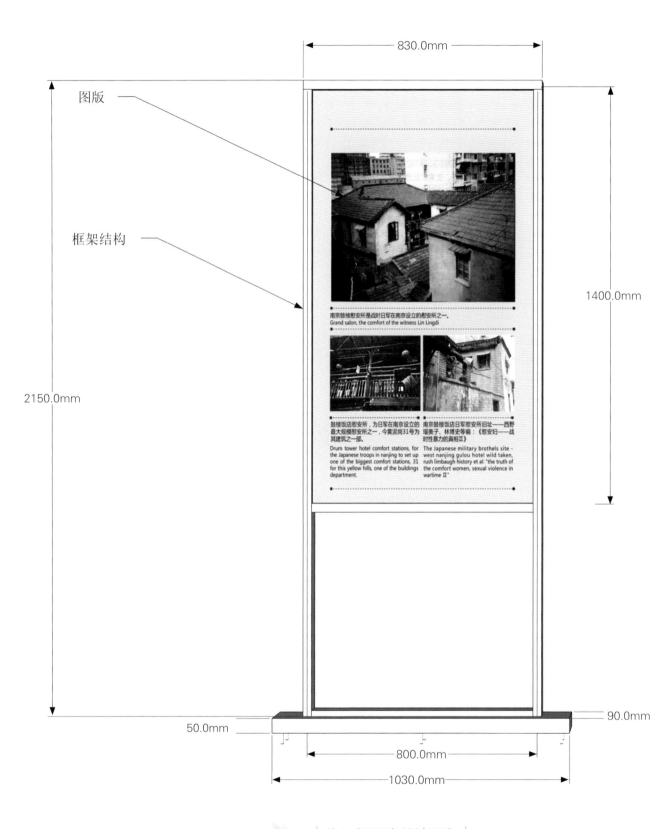

| 独立式图版架设计图稿 |

| 室内展陈　INDOOR EXHIBITION |

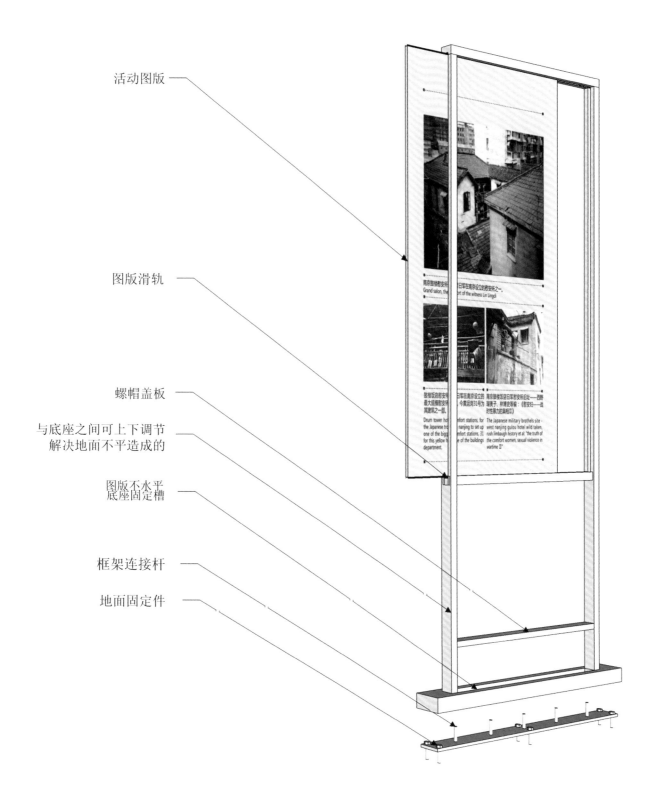

▶ 独立式图版架设计图稿

室内展陈　INDOOR EXHIBITION

一级文物——内窥器展示

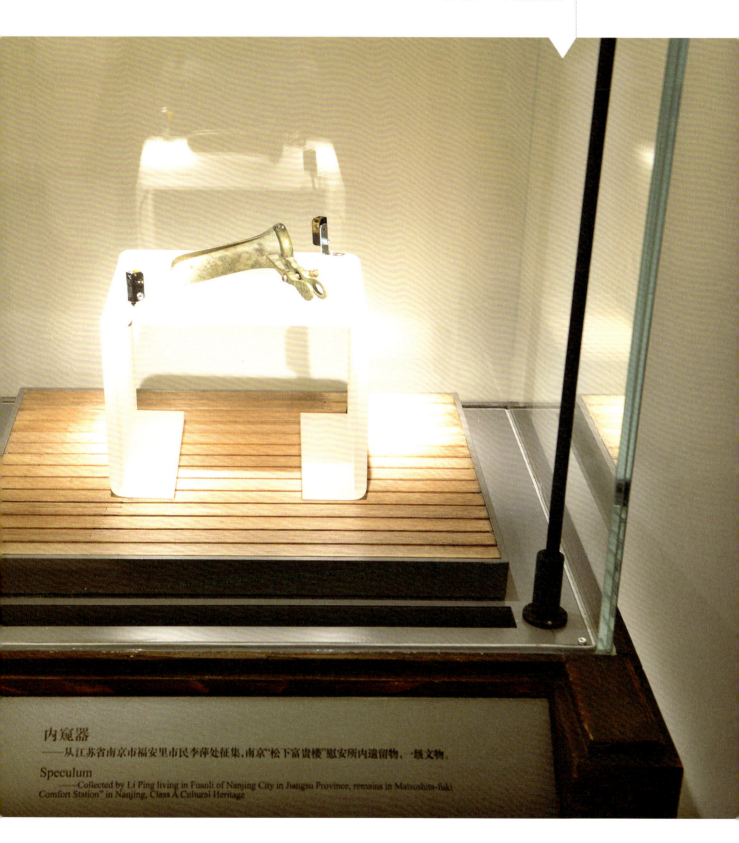

内窥器
——从江苏省南京市福安里市民李萍处征集,南京"松下富贵楼"慰安所内遗留物,一级文物。

Speculum
——Collected by Li Ping living in Fuanli of Nanjing City in Jiangsu Province, remains in Matsushita-fuki Comfort Station" in Nanjing, Class A Cultural Heritage

利济巷慰安所遗留物展示

室内展陈　INDOOR EXHIBITION

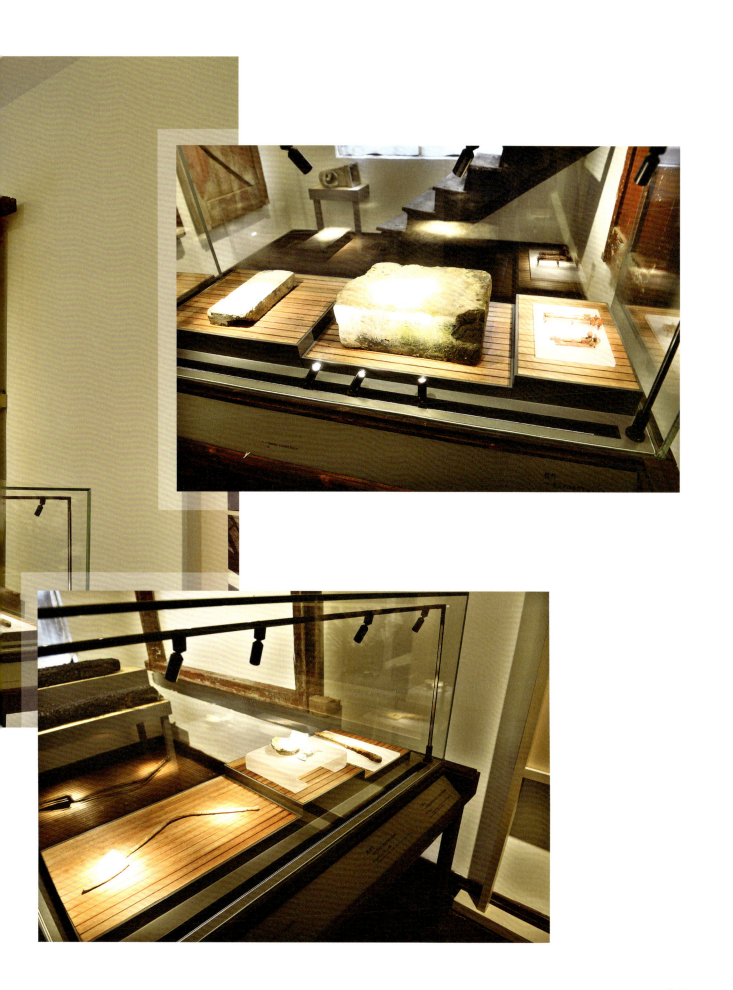

"慰安妇"幸存者
雷桂英遗留物展示

"慰安妇"幸存者雷桂英遗留物展示

| 室内展陈　INDOOR EXHIBITION |

一级文物——消毒剂"高锰酸钾"
("慰安妇"幸存者雷桂英捐赠)

| 室内展陈 INDOOR EXHIBITION

101

韩籍"慰安妇"
朴永心指认房间

| 室内展陈　INDOOR EXHIBITION |

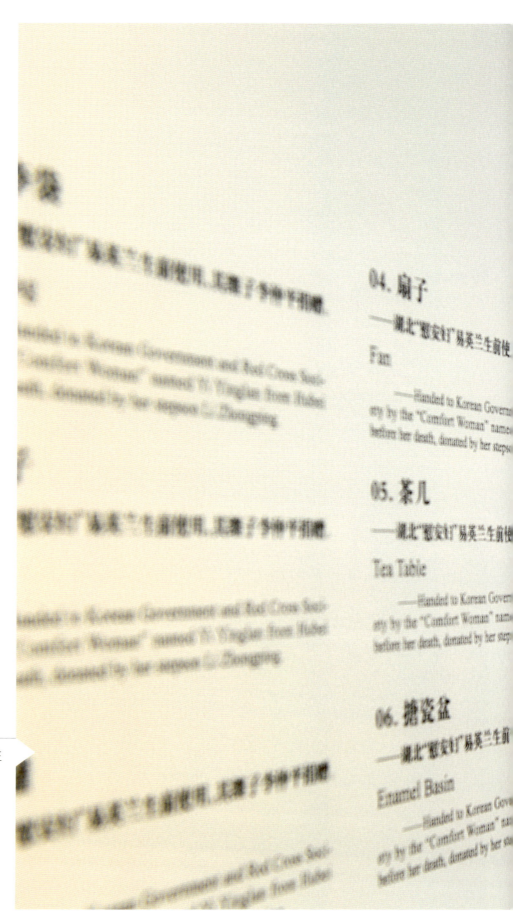

"慰安妇"幸存者易英兰遗留物展示

室内展陈　INDOOR EXHIBITION

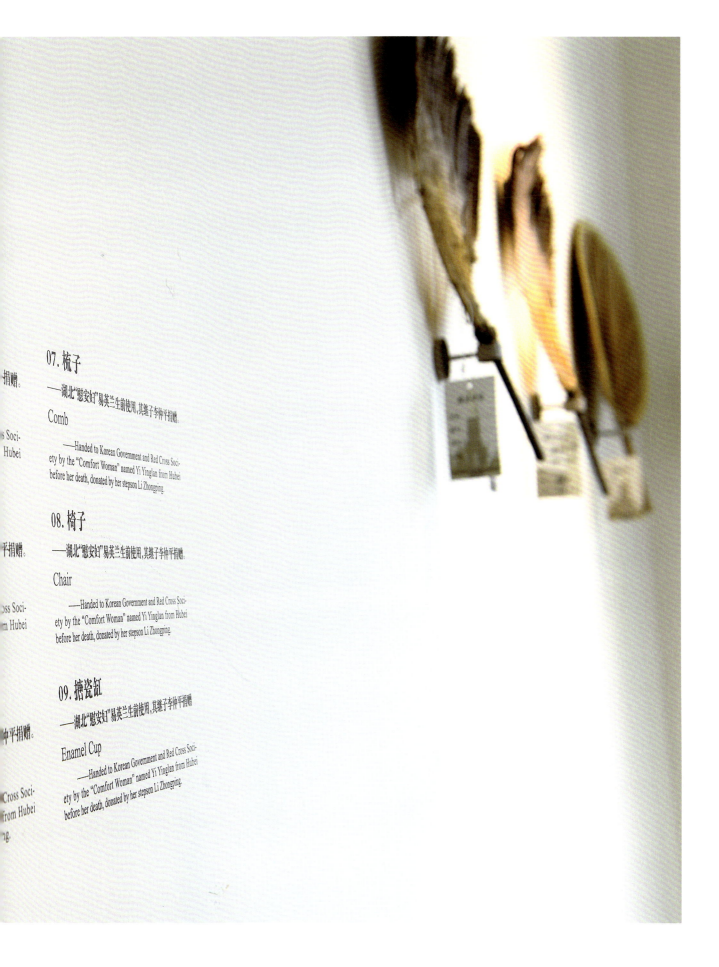

07. 梳子
——湖北"慰安妇"易英兰生前使用，其继子李仲平捐赠。

Comb
——Handed to Korean Government and Red Cross Society by the "Comfort Woman" named Yi Yinglan from Hubei before her death, donated by her stepson Li Zhongping.

08. 椅子
——湖北"慰安妇"易英兰生前使用，其继子李仲平捐赠。

Chair
——Handed to Korean Government and Red Cross Society by the "Comfort Woman" named Yi Yinglan from Hubei before her death, donated by her stepson Li Zhongping.

09. 搪瓷缸
——湖北"慰安妇"易英兰生前使用，其继子李仲平捐赠

Enamel Cup
——Handed to Korean Government and Red Cross Society by the "Comfort Woman" named Yi Yinglan from Hubei before her death, donated by her stepson Li Zhongping.

室内展陈 INDOOR EXHIBITION

"慰安妇"幸存者
易英兰遗留物展示

107

| C区专题陈列 THEME EXHIBITION IN AREA C |

专题陈列由沪城性奴泪、遍布中国的日军慰安所、伤痛记忆与控诉、众多国籍的性奴隶四部分内容组成，分别介绍了上海、中国、朝鲜半岛、东南亚、太平洋诸岛等地区日军慰安所及"慰安妇"的史实内容。它们是基本陈列的重要补充，以更加翔实的史料与文物来揭露那段黑暗的历史。

The theme exhibition is composed of four parts, which are "The Tears of Sex Slaves in Shanghai", "Japanese Comfort Houses Scattered all over China", "Painful Memory and Denouncement" and "Sex Slaves from Various Nations". They showed the historical records of Japanese "comfort houses" and "comfort women" ranging from Shanghai, China, Korean peninsula, Southeast Asia and various island on Pacific oceans. They supplemented the basic exhibition and used more detailed historical records and relics to uncover the tragic period of history.

| 室内展陈 INDOOR EXHIBITION |

沪城性奴泪
展厅空间

室内展陈 INDOOR EXHIBITION

室内展陈 INDOOR EXHIBITION

沪城性奴泪文物展示

室内展陈 INDOOR EXHIBITION

沪城性奴泪文物展示

室内展陈　INDOOR EXHIBITION

到上海的女性在这里接受体检,合格者进入了杨家宅慰安所。 ——(日)《一亿人的昭和史》

Women who came to Shanghai from other places received physical checkups here, and the qualified were sent into the Yangjiazhai "Comfort Station".
——(Japan) *Showa History of 100 Million People*

慰安所体检台
复制品展示

遍布中国的
日军慰安所
展示空间

室内展陈　INDOOR EXHIBITION

慰安所遗留物场景复原展示

遍布中国的日军慰安所图文展示

室内展陈　INDOOR EXHIBITION

▶ 67位日军"慰安妇"幸存者群像设计稿

121

慰安所遗留物
场景复原展示

室内展陈 INDOOR EXHIBITION

慰安所遗留物场景复原展示

室内展陈　INDOOR EXHIBITION

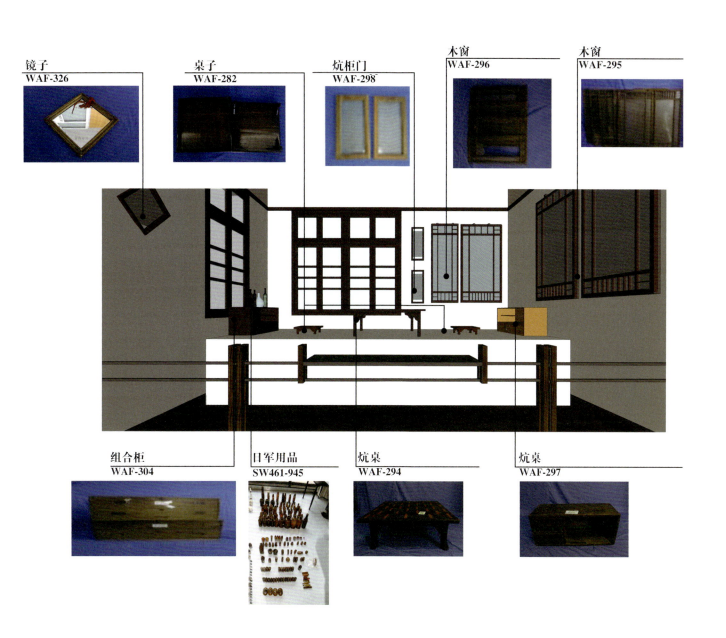

▶ 慰安所遗留物场景复原展示设计稿

伤痛记忆与控诉展示空间

室内展陈 INDOOR EXHIBITION

126

对日军"慰安妇"制度罪行的控诉

ACCUSATIONS AGAINST CRIMES ON "COMFORT WOMEN" SYSTEM COMMITTED BY THE JAPANESE ARMY

日本軍「慰安婦」制度の罪行に対する告訴

일본군 '위안부' 제도 죄행에 대한 공소

1990年11月,以韩国梨花大学教授尹贞玉为首的"韩国女子挺身队问题对策协议会"正式成立,从事有关日军"慰安妇"历史研究和传播。在韩国民众的呼吁下,当时的总统卢泰愚下令对战时韩国女子被迫充当日军"慰安妇"历史展开全面调查。韩国民间捐款为"慰安妇"幸存者设立了"分享之家",建立日军"慰安妇"历史馆。

On November 1990, Yoon Geong-ok, professor at Ewha Women's University of South Korea, led to the creation of the Korean Council for the Women Drafted for Military Slavery by Japan, focusing on the research and spread of the "Comfort Women" history.Urged by Korean people, then the Korean President Roh Tae-woo gave the order to carry out a full investigation on the "Comfort Women" crime.The "House of Sharing", a shelter for living "Comfort Women", was founded through funds raised by South Korean civic groups and the Museum of Sexual Slavery by Japanese Military was also established.

1990年11月、韓国梨花大学の尹貞玉教授を始め「韓国挺身隊問題対策協会」が正式に成立し、日本軍「慰安婦」の歴史に関する研究と宣伝を行います。韓国民衆の声の中で、当時の大統領盧泰愚氏は、戦時韓国女性が日本軍「慰安婦」にされた歴史について全面調査する指令を出しました。韓国は民間募金で「慰安婦」生存者のために「シェアハウス」を設立し、日本軍「慰安婦」歴史館を設置しました。

1990년 11월 한국이화여대 교수 윤정옥을 대표로 한 '한국정신대문제대책협의회'가 성식으로 설립되어 일본군 '위안부' 관련 역사 연구와 전파에 종사하였다. 한국 민중들의 호소 하에 당시 대통령 노태우는 2차대전 기간 한국 여성이 강제로 일본군 '위안부'로 전락된 역사에 대해 전면적인 조사를 진행하도록 지시하였다. 한국 민간에서는 '위안부' 생존자들을 위한 헌금으로 '나눔의 집'을 설립하고 일본군 '위안부' 역사관을 건립하였다.

| 图版设计稿 |

伤痛记忆与控诉文物展示

室内展陈　INDOOR EXHIBITION

袖扣
WAF-167

袖扣
WAF-170

头饰
WAF-176

裤子标牌
WAF-169

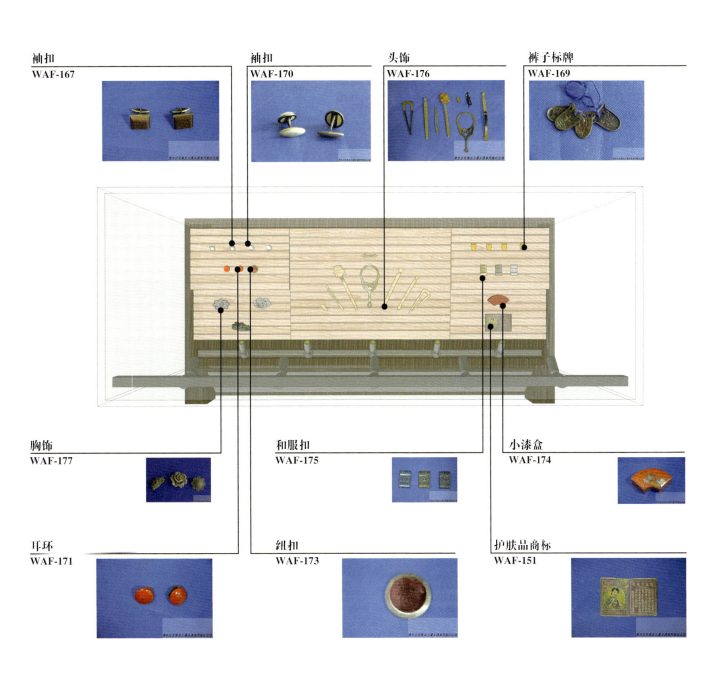

胸饰
WAF-177

和服扣
WAF-175

小漆盒
WAF-174

耳环
WAF-171

纽扣
WAF-173

护肤品商标
WAF-151

▶ 展柜柜内设计稿

129

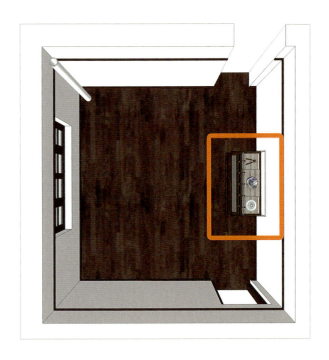

| 展柜室内顶面图 |

| 伤痛记忆与控诉
文物展示 |

| 室内展陈　INDOOR EXHIBITION |

理发推子	青花瓷碗	香水瓶
WAF-358	**WAF-252**	**WAF-361**

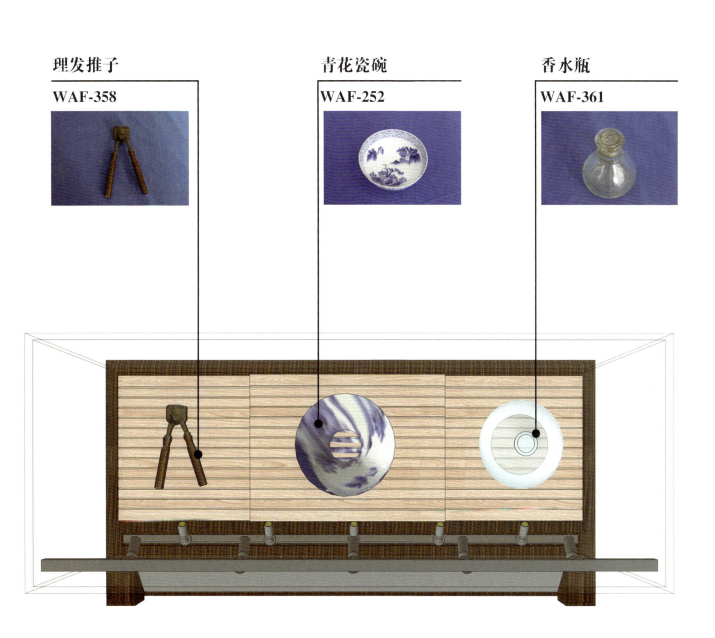

▶ 展柜柜内设计稿

伤痛记忆与控诉文物展示

| 展柜室内顶面图 |

| 室内展陈　INDOOR EXHIBITION |

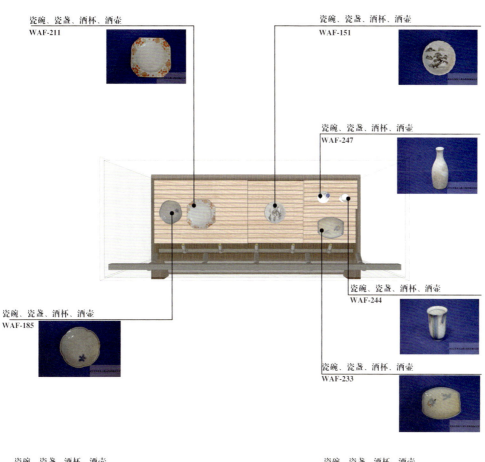

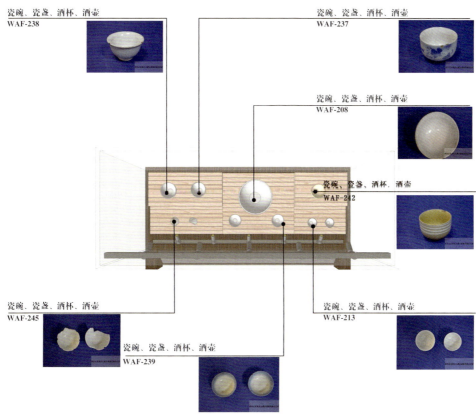

▶ | 展柜柜内设计稿 |

众多国籍的性奴隶文物场景展示

室内展陈 INDOOR EXHIBITION

"慰安妇"
雕塑展示

《黎明之眼》海报
The Poster of The Eyes of Dawn

室内展陈 INDOOR EXHIBITION

137

建 设 历 程
THE CONSTRUCTION PROCESS

南京利济巷慰安所旧址陈列馆展陈设计施工一体化工程前后历时半年，时间紧、任务重。但爱涛人积极发扬勇于开拓、敢为人先的精神，攻坚克难，按时保质地完成了任务。

The design and construction of Nanjing Museum of Site of Lijixiang Comfort Stations has lasted for half a year. Time is limited but the task is heavy. However, we Artallers, with adventurous and pioneering spirit, have overcome difficulties and finished the task on time with satisfying quality.

建设历程一览表

工程前期

投标设计

2014年11月
利济巷慰安所旧址的修缮保护、陈列布展工作启动

2015年5月
5月1日，利济巷慰安所旧址修缮改造工程正式开工建设

2015年6月
6月初利济巷慰安所旧址陈列布展工程投标设计

6月底利济巷慰安所旧址陈列布展工程投标设计成功中标

2015年7月
7月15日利济巷慰安所旧址陈列布展工程设计交底会

建设历程　THE CONSTRUCTION PROCESS

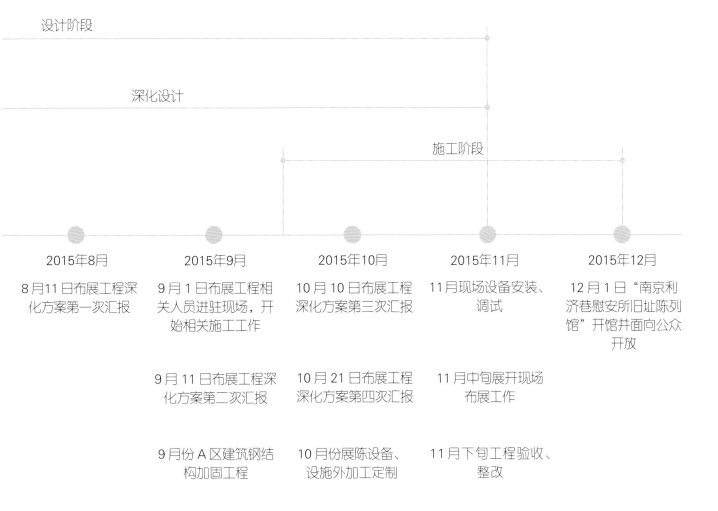

▶ 建设历程会议纪要

建设历程 THE CONSTRUCTION PROCESS

| 建设历程会议纪要 |

建设历程　THE CONSTRUCTION PROCESS

勘查现场

旧址建筑结构加固

旧址建筑结构加固

| 建设历程 THE CONSTRUCTION PROCESS |

建设施工现场

▶ 设计团队现场设计方案

建设历程 THE CONSTRUCTION PROCESS

施工现场室外"泪滴墙"安装

建设历程　THE CONSTRUCTION PROCESS

施工现场布展

151

媒体报道摘录

MEDIA REPORTS
EXTRACT

扬子晚报 12月02日

泪洒满墙,历史是最好的"清醒剂"

利济巷慰安所旧址陈列馆昨开馆
为魂串起全部展陈

前事不忘 泪洒"一面墙"

控诉声声 历史是最好的"清醒剂"

陈列了什么 以五个"泪"为魂串起全部展陈

回望 保住这处历史遗址 学者曾断指拆迁办封条

南京大屠杀死难者 遗属举办"家祭"

将来 明年3月将再次 提交慰安妇申遗材料

■小贴士 陈列馆每天接待200名观众

徐州市食品药品监管局从早餐集中整治入手 大力整顿规范全市餐饮市场监管秩序

扬子晚报12月30日 YANGZI EVENING NEWS DECEMBER 30TH

爱涛文化奉献利济巷慰安所旧址陈列馆

媒体报道摘录 MEDIA REPORTS EXTRACT

"利济巷"经历艰难路径,终不负期待

| 南京日报12月13日 |

以泪为魂，讲述"慰安妇"泣血历史

"五串泪"撑起整个展陈

冬日凛冽寒风中，八栋灰黄色建筑静静伫立，无声地向世人诉说着侵华日军的罪行。

12月1日，南京利济巷慰安所旧址陈列馆举行开馆仪式并试运行。作为侵华日军南京大屠杀遇难同胞纪念馆的分馆，这里是中国大陆首座经"慰安妇"亲自指认的、以"慰安妇"为主题的纪念馆。

陈列馆以泪为魂，固化"慰安妇"的血泪记忆，它留给人们的是历史的启迪与对和平的思考。

以"泪滴"表现磨难，反映"慰安妇"的悲怆状态

在挂有"南京利济巷慰安所旧址陈列馆"牌子的外墙上，悬挂十几颗由铝品制成的巨大"泪滴"，晶莹剔透。

"设计过程中，究竟采用什么元素反映'慰安妇'这一特殊题材更为合适？为此，我们提出了用诸如枯萎的花朵、泪滴、镣铐的笔墨等元素串起整个陈展。"陈列馆设计单位、江苏紫涛文化产业有限公司的设计总监任睿说，经与当时的侵华日军南京大屠杀遇难同胞纪念馆馆长、利济巷慰安所旧址维修保护和陈列布展

工程专家组组长朱成山再三商榷，最终选定泪滴作为主要元素，"泪滴采来表现个体受到的磨难相对比较贴切，尤其是反映慰安妇的那种愁怨状态。"

在此基础上，结合环境空间，朱成山提出了从墙上到地下有关泪滴的创意。

"泪洒一面墙"——当年"慰安妇"们恐怖的眼泪洒落在慰安所内每个角落。虚妄陈旧的砖地上，仿佛可见墙大的泪滴，折射出她们的无助与绝望。

"泪滴一片地"——一面巨大的黑白照片墙上，是"慰安妇"一张张饱经岁月风霜的面孔，有的人在仰天呐喊，有的人在低头抹泪；照片墙下方，是一块湿漉漉的土地。时间的车轮虽然过去了半个多世纪，"慰安妇"老泪纵横的泪水依然流淌着浸湿了地面，这是对日军实施"慰安妇"制度罪行无言的控诉。

"泪滴一条路"——窗井盖上是一滴滴晶莹形状，高悬着"慰安妇"们痛苦的泪水，曾经把她们哭喊地洒落在慰安所内一条路上。

序厅"无言的泪"，仿佛"慰安妇"们的眼泪悬在头顶

序厅"无言的泪"，让观众进入展厅的第一视角就有泪的震撼。

在A区基本陈列序厅中间的顶部，悬挂着一圈圈的"慰安妇"照片，最下方的中间用泪滴汇集组成团，像"慰安妇"的眼泪悬挂于头顶之上。

"与绝大多数纪念馆不同，陈列馆的序厅有六七米高，但面积只有40平方米，给我们发挥的余地比较局促。"任睿说，为此，他们做了一个大胆的设计，让观众抬头就能看见，头顶有很多"慰安妇"的照片被铁链缠绕在一起，她们在里面苦苦挣扎，令人触目。

"铁丝网寓意战争与罪恶的'慰安妇'制度，好似龙卷风一般将无数原本过着平和生活的女孩卷入血腥的阴云里。"朱成山说，在形似尊崇的尽头，可见到的侵华日军在华设立的各所慰安所名录，印证着可恶可耻的"慰安妇"制度的暴行，不容忽略。

陈列馆以黑白灰为基调，连辅助展示设备、材料都给人陈旧的感觉。

"之前有些已经破损的门窗也全部加固以复新安装上去的，连展柜都是经过涂抹的，这是我们专门订制的，蕴含浴火重生的意思。"任睿说，在设计过程中，尽量减少使用金属、玻璃等现代材料，"即使安装消防、喷淋、监控、灯具等设施，我们也统一安装进入金属片架，以便于在墙上凿开，以最大限度地保持它的原貌。"

铜雕"流不尽的泪"，让观众去擦拭时感同身受

利济巷慰安所旧址陈列馆。

在A区基本陈列序厅的尾部，一件名为"流不尽的泪"的雕塑让人看了心酸，与序厅中"无言的泪"形成首尾呼应。

铜雕的"慰安妇"老人用力从墙体里挣脱出半个身子，她的表情异常痛苦，眼泪不停地流出，触心的观众可以拿起放置在一旁的手帕为老人拭去脸上的泪水，然而刚刚擦过，不久又会有泪从老人眼中流出来。

"无言的泪"和"流不尽的泪"也是朱馆长提出来的创意。我们原本想制作一个片子在这里播映，里面是很多"慰安妇"在哭泣的场景。但这种表现方式比较直白，艺术的感觉可能不够，朱馆长让我们在序厅中间做个"泪团"，在尾厅做一个铜雕，与观众形成互动，让大家为铜雕擦眼泪，有种感同身受的感觉。"任睿向记者透露了"流不尽的泪"的秘密：原来铜

雕里面有一个水循环系统，它慢慢地蓄满水，出口就在两个眼眶的地方。"蓄满之后水就会往外涌，不过就停留在涌的阶段，雕体之后又会重新涌出来。"

"'慰安妇'是一个非常特殊的群体，不仅在被加害时流泪，即便幸存下来，在以后的几十年生活里，她们也活在痛苦的回忆之中，一生都有流不尽的泪，像如泉水、如泉水，最后泪槽都泣尽了。"朱成山说，鉴此拉意，陈列馆以"泪"为魂，设计了"泪滴一面墙"、"泪滴一片地"、"泪滴一条路"，以及A区展览"无言的泪"和"流不尽的泪"五大部分，串起整个展陈，以此记录"慰安妇"受害者的这段血泪历史。"尽管我国申报的'慰安妇'档案申遗撼地落选，但是，'慰安妇'的血泪记忆不容忘却，只有正视历史，以史为鉴，才能开创和平未来。"

一位参观的市民正用手巾为陈列馆内展示的雕塑《流不尽的泪》擦拭眼泪。

南京利济巷慰安所旧址陈列馆

南京利济巷慰安所旧址由8栋民国时期的历史建筑组成，原由国民党中将杨普庆于1935年至1937年间陆续兴建，为两层砖木混合结构的建筑群，名"普庆新村"。1937年底，日军占领南京后，将利济巷2号改为"东云慰安所"，将18号改为"故乡楼慰安所"。

2003年11月，朝鲜籍"慰安妇"朴永心老人首来现场指认。2004年6月，这里的住户唐过迁走，"拆"字落下。2008年冬季节，烟花爆竹引发大火，建筑破损严重，有识之士呼吁抢救。经过保护，成了投诉中的站点。2014年11月，侵华日军南京利济巷慰安所旧址维修保护和陈列布展工程正式开工建设，2015年5月1日，利济巷慰安所旧址维修改

造工程正式开工建设，2015年12月正式对外开放。

南京利济巷慰安所旧址陈列馆占地3680平方米，8栋建筑面积3412平方米，展陈面积约3000平方米，整个陈列分为基本陈列、旧址陈列和中心专题陈列，包括《战争性奴隶性制度》、《琼瑶罗魔》、《护城性奴隶性》、《魂牵中国的日军'慰安妇'》、《传播记忆与控诉》、《众多国籍的性奴隶》，全面介绍了侵华日军"慰安妇"制度的起源、确立与实行过程，中国、朝鲜半岛、东南亚及太平洋诸海岛等地的慰安所，以及遗留南京等日军"慰安妇"问题与相关历史记忆，共展出照片680多张，文物1600多件，视频19部。

陈列馆外墙上的泪滴造型雕塑。

| 南京晨报 12月2日 |

A04 | 晨报看点

2015年12月2日 星期三

慰安所交易的筹码。 新华报业视觉中心记者 万程鹏 余萍 摄

展馆前的雕塑。 新华报业视觉中心记者 吴俊 摄

展馆内陈列的文物展品。 新华报业视觉中心记者 邵丹 摄

南京利济巷慰安所旧址陈列馆开馆

这是中国大陆首座以慰安妇为主题的纪念馆

眼泪流淌成河，浸润了脚下的泥土，这空间里满载的屈辱和悲伤，伴随了她们一辈子。位于南京利济巷2号的8幢小楼，在12月1日，以南京利济巷慰安所旧址陈列馆的身份再次向世人开启。作为侵华日军南京大屠杀遇难同胞纪念馆的分馆，这里是中国大陆首座经慰安妇亲自指认的以慰安妇为主题的纪念馆。昨天上午中宣部以及省市领导、各界群众等300多人出席开馆仪式。

一滴滴"泪滴"
折射慰安妇的无助与绝望

南京利济巷慰安所旧址陈列馆由八幢两层建筑组成，总建筑面积3000多平方米。其中六幢为展陈馆，两幢为办公楼。修葺之前的利济巷2号建筑一度残破不堪，翻新后的利济巷也并不新。外围一圈灰色栏杆，取代了原本的砖石围墙，外墙保留了原本棕黄偏暗的底色。曾经残破缺失的窗户及门基本被修葺，窗框和门里偏暗的棕红色。一幢建筑外墙正面上覆盖着70位当年的慰安妇幸存者的黑白肖像照片。照片墙下一块湿土将"终年湿润"，象征受害者的眼泪永不会干涸。

在有着"南京利济巷慰安所旧址陈列馆"标识的外墙上，挂着十几颗由铅晶制成的巨大"泪滴"，寓意着"泪流一面墙"，当年慰安妇们悲伤的眼泪，不经意间挥洒在慰安所内每个角落。斑驳陈旧的墙面上，仿佛可见硕大的泪滴，折射出她们的无助与绝望。

据了解，南京利济巷慰安所旧址，由原国民党中将杨普庆于1935年至1937年间陆续建造，为两层砖木混合结构的建筑物，名为"普庆新村"。1937年底，日军占领南京之后，将利济巷2号改造为"东云慰安所"，将18号改造为"故乡楼慰安所"。

一座雕塑
她的遭遇发生在这里

顺着流淌的"泪滴"而下，一座铜质塑像震撼人心，塑像主体是三位慰安妇，一位跪地披散着头发，一位扶着孕肚抚摸慰安妇跪地的妇女，另一位挽着其中一位之手掩面哭泣。三人相互依偎的无助造型令人心疼。

雕塑中那位怀孕妇女的原型就是朝鲜籍慰安妇朴永心，1939年她被日军以招工之名骗至中国南京，在利济巷2号日军东云慰安所做慰安妇长达三年时间。1944年，朴永心怀着身孕与另外3名朝鲜籍慰安妇被送出战壕时，被中国远征军解救出来，并由美国随军记者拍摄了著名的二战照片《怀孕的慰安妇》。1945年9月底，朴永心被遣返回国。2003年11月，朴永心以年老抱病之身重返中国，实地查证当年受难之地——南京和腾冲松山，完成了她至死也要控诉日军罪行的心愿。她指认的当年被拘禁的地方——利济巷2号楼上第19号房间，就位于现在南京利济巷慰安所旧址陈列馆内。

一份份铁证
控诉着侵华日军罪恶行径

陈列馆共展出了1600多件文物展品、400多块图板、680多幅照片，其中两件国家一级文物显得尤为珍贵。一件是已故慰安妇雷桂英老人生前捐赠的消毒剂高锰酸钾，这些大颗粒的高锰酸钾是南京汤山原日军高台坡慰安所发给慰安妇用作卫生措施的。另一件是松下富贵楼慰安所为慰安妇检查身体时使用的内窥器。此外，还有从日本友人大东仁处征集的"突击一番"安全套和星秘膏。1938年2月19日，日军华中派遣宪兵队司令官大木繁《关于南京宪兵辖区治安恢复状况的调查报告（通牒）》，汇总了1938年2月1日至10日南京及周边地区各市县军队"慰安实施"状况。其中南京有驻军兵25000人，有慰安妇141名，平均一个慰安妇应对的士兵数是178。

"流不尽的泪"雕塑。 新华报业视觉中心记者 邵丹 摄

声音
亲属讲述
老人生前心路历程

捐赠者之一的唐家国今年58岁，居住在江宁区汤山镇，由于要来参加这次陈列馆开馆，甚至没来得及吃早饭。唐家国是雷桂英老人的养子，雷桂英是南京目前唯一公开自己受害经历的慰安妇。据了解，他这次将雷桂英老人生前遗留的床、(消毒用)高锰酸钾等一些可以作为历史见证的物件都捐给了纪念馆。

"她走的时候是这样讲的，日本人不承认，那么就算是我死了，我还有儿子，我有物证，儿子也可以帮我打这个官司。她有这个心愿，就算自己去不了，儿子也要去，如果有可能要去日本打官司。她很坚强，一般人可能承受不了的她都承受住了。"据唐家国回忆，老人生前曾因为子女的原因并不打算将自己的亲身经历说出来，"我劝过她，她说，'这样会丢脸的'。我说，为了死难者，你要把它说出来。你不说出来，将来人们就不知道了。"

唐家国的女儿女婿及全家人也很支持，"叫奶奶说出来吧"，经儿孙做思想工作，终于在2006年老人接受了媒体的采访。老人于2007年4月25日去世。

幸存者迫于压力
往往不愿承认

现年72岁的姜伟勋，家住如皋市白蒲镇杨家围村，走路略显蹒跚的他，也带着儿子儿媳来到了利济巷陈列馆，捐赠了周粉英老人生前的遗物。周粉英老人的孙子姜国平坦承奶奶以前不想把这件事情说出来，自从听闻雷桂英老人的遭遇后，奶奶才勇敢地站出来。"我希望国人铭记历史，勿让悲剧重演。一个中国人被日本人欺负了，如果不说出来，后代人就不会知道，希望让国人更清醒地了解这段历史真相。"

上海师范大学教授苏智良在采访中表示："纪念馆中有日本老兵的回忆，有受害者到现场指证的记录，它增加了历史的证据。日本某些人特别是某些政治家是毫无道理的，他们拿不出任何证据，如果他们到这里来看，看他们是否还能坚持那种谬论。当然我们需找证据还应当联合其他国家，为慰安妇档案申请世界记忆名录。"据了解，虽然近些年有媒体的宣传，国人更加宽容了，但仍有一部分幸存者不愿意承认自己曾经是慰安妇。

70位当年慰安妇幸存者的黑白肖像照片墙。 刘建华 摄 (VIJS供图)

揭秘
罪恶的"樱花票"
新街口一带曾有多个慰安所

"其实除了利济巷，新街口一带有多处当年日军的慰安所，像铁管巷四达里就是其中之一，距离利济巷很近。"南京地方志办公室研究人员胡卓然在接受记者采访时，披露了关于慰安所一些鲜为人知的历史。

"南京沦陷后不到半年，1938年6月11日《烽火》杂志第17期刊发了南京大屠杀幸存者李伟涛的回忆文章《樱花票》，这也是最早揭露日寇于南京设置慰安所的幸存者见证之一。"胡卓然告诉记者，文中曾有这样的记录："掳去的女人，自然是供他兽兵泄欲的。可是这泄欲也并不单纯的，一方面她们还成了敌拿敛财的机会。这就是说：她们是被编为随营娼妓了，铁管巷四达里(或是道上里)，那数十间新造的房子，且成了随营娼妓的总部。"

据这篇文章记载，虽然是慰安所，但士兵们不是能随便出入的，"他们想泄欲的话，要到'樱花办事处'去登记，缴纳一定的价值领到那张'樱花票'后，再根据那号码的所示，找寻那相同号码的女人。随营妓女不能拒绝来泄欲的兽兵的，就是敌兵，也没有自由来选一个女人。而且如果这敌兵第二次来寻欢时必然是一个和上次不同的号码，据说，这样是防止敌兵诱娼妓嬉惑，而泄了秘密。"

"如果士兵需要泄欲但身上没钱，'樱花办事处'甚至可以采用记账的方式，只要有兽号证明，在勇票根上签个字，就一样得到一张'樱花票'，然后'樱花办事处'就报告士兵所属的部队，并在领发军饷时扣除。而'樱花办事处'收入的，也是他们军需处收入的一项正宗，士卒们所得的军饷，其实大部分仍被吸收回去。"胡卓然说，随营妓每天要被支配蹂躏五次以上，一天只有三餐，此外就只有管理人的鞭挞了，"若被掳去的女人不服从'樱花办事处'的管理和支配时，悲惨境遇是我们无法想象的。《樱花票》里就记录了一件残酷的事，有一次一个士兵去泄欲被拒绝，管理员就对那女人施以惨绝人寰的毒打，结果那个士兵也不忍见那惨状，将毒打者刺死，后来这个士兵也被军部处了死刑。可见日寇毫无人性。" 朱家齐 记者 黄欢 周晶

公司荣誉

GLORIES

十多年的行业深耕，不仅锻炼出一支经验丰富、素质过硬的专业设计团队，更打造了数量众多的行业精品项目，并多次获得行业各类奖项。

Over ten years of industry experience have not only witnessed the development of an experienced and professional design team but also a great number of refined projects that have won various awards.

2010年上海世界博览会江苏省主题馆
Jiangsu theme pavilion in Shanghai World Expo 2010

陕西历史博物馆基本陈列《陕西古代文明》以第一名的成绩荣获全国博物馆十大陈列展览精品奖
Basic exhibit of *Shaanxi Ancient Civilization* was awarded Excellent Prize of national museum top ten exhibitions

山西博物院——晋魂展示陈列荣获全国博物馆十大陈列展览精品奖
Shanxi Museum—soul of jin dynasty exhibition was awarded Excellent Prize of national museum top ten exhibitions

甘肃省博物馆——博物馆基本陈列荣获全国博物馆十大陈列展览精品奖
Gansu Museum—basic exhibit was awarded Excellent Prize of national museum top ten exhibitions

八路军太行纪念馆——八路军抗战史基本陈列荣获全国博物馆十大陈列展览特别奖
The Eighth Route Army Taihang Memorial Hall—basic exhibit of the history of the eighth route army was awarded Special Prize of national museum top ten exhibitions

南京市博物馆——"龙蟠虎踞"陈列展示荣获全国博物馆十大陈列展览提名奖
Nanjing Municipal Museum—exhibit of "a coiling dragon and a crouching tiger" won a nomination of national museum top ten exhibitions

南京博物院展示陈列荣获国家文物局全国年度"十大精品工程奖"
Exhibition in Nanjing Museum was awarded by State Administration of Cultural Heritage the national top ten excellent projects

武汉博物馆展示陈列荣获国家文物局全国年度"十大精品工程奖"
Exhibition in Wuhan Museum was awarded by State Administration of Cultural Heritage the national top ten excellent projects

无锡钱钟书纪念馆展示陈列入围国家文物局全国年度"十大精品工程奖"
Exhibition of Wuxi Qian Zhongshu Memorial was a candidate for the national top ten excellent projects selected by State Administration of Cultural Heritage

江苏省首届文化艺术精品展示陈列设计入围国家文物局全国年度"十大精品工程奖"
Exhibition of the First Cultural and Art Exhibition in Jiangsu Province was a candidate for the national top ten excellent projects selected by State Administration of Cultural Heritage

皖风徽韵——文房四宝荣获全国十大陈列展览精品奖
Anhui Style and Charm-- the "scholar's four jewels" was awarded the national top ten excellent exhibitions

南京博物院
Nanjing Museum

后　　记

  项目作为第二个国家公祭日相关活动的重要组成，同时作为铭刻历史记忆、控诉日军暴行的重要证据，其意义非比寻常。在南京市委、市政府有关领导的高度关心下，在时任侵华日军南京大屠杀遇难同胞纪念馆朱成山馆长的全面统筹下，在南京大学建筑设计院和南京市城建集团项目工程公司的大力支持下，由任睿设计团队负责项目的概念设计、深化设计和布展设计的展陈整体设计布展工作，前后历时数月，方案几经修改、完善，向国家、向人民、向社会交出了一份圆满的答卷，陈列馆于2015年12月1日正式向社会开放。

  本书从最初设想，到付梓印刷，《泪滴塑空间：南京利济巷慰安所旧址陈列馆展陈艺术图集》历时半年多终与读者见面。此图册介绍了展陈设计工作之始末，记录了所有项目人员之付出，留存了那段历史的宝贵记忆，更记载下策展人和设计师心路之历程。谨以此书的出版作为纪念，让更多人了解那段鲜为人知的历史伤痛，也为了警醒我们珍爱今日来之不易的和平与幸福。

  在本书编撰、编印的过程中得到了集团公司的重视和支持。朱成山馆长代为作序，并给予指导与帮助；此外，东南大学出版社的相关老师对本书的编辑、出版给予了众多建议及大力支持，在此谨表示衷心感谢。

2016年10月20日

AFTERWORD

As an important component of the series activities of the second National Memorial Day, meanwhile as an important evidence to engrave historical memory and to condemn Japanese army's atrocities, this project is of the unusual significance. Highly concerned by the leaders of Nanjing Municipal Government and CPC Nanjing Committee, with the comprehensive co-ordination by Mr. Zhu Chengshan, the director of the Memorial Hall of the Victims in Nanjing Massacre by Japanese Invaders, and with the support of the Institute of Architecture Design & Planning of Nanjing University and Nanjing Urban Construction Project Construction Management Co., the concept design, detailed design and exhibition design were accomplished by Ren Rui Designing Team, who is responsible for the overall exhibition design. With several months' effort, after the plan was modified and improved for many times, we have finally delivered a satisfactory answer to the country and the people. On December 1st, 2015, the museum officially opened to the public.

From the initial idea, to being sent to print, which lasted for half a year, Tears Sculpture Space—Nanjing Museum of Site of Lijixiang Comfort Stations Art Atlas Exhibit has been eventually published. This atlas introduces the whole process of exhibition design, records the work of all project personnel, preserves the precious historic memory, and records the mental experiences of the curator and the designers. The publication of this atlas is a souvenir to mark the first anniversary of Nanjing Museum of Site of Lijixiang Comfort Stations, which may not only let more people understand the pain of this little-known history, but also remind us to cherish the hard-earned peace and happiness.

The compilation and publication of this atlas got much attention and support from the group company Director Zhu Chengshan wrote the preface, and gave guidance and help. In addition, the editors of Southeast University Press, has given a lot of suggestions and support to the edition and publication of the book. We'd like to express our sincere gratitude.

October 20, 2016

图书在版编目（CIP）数据

泪滴塑空间：南京利济巷慰安所旧址陈列馆展陈艺术图集 / 朱成山，任睿主编 . — 南京：东南大学出版社，2017.6
　ISBN 978-7-5641-7087-5

　Ⅰ. ①泪… Ⅱ. ①朱… ②任… Ⅲ. ①军国主义 - 性犯罪 - 史料 - 日本 Ⅳ. ① K313.46

中国版本图书馆CIP数据核字（2017）第 058664 号

书　　　名：泪滴塑空间：南京利济巷慰安所旧址陈列馆展陈艺术图集
责任编辑：丁　丁
责任印制：周荣虎

出版发行：东南大学出版社
社　　　址：南京市四牌楼2号　邮编：210096
出　版　人：江建中
网　　　址：http://www.seupress.com

印　　　刷：上海雅昌艺术印刷有限公司
开　　　本：889mm×1194mm　1/16
印　　　张：11.375
字　　　数：389 千
版　　　次：2017 年 6 月第 1 版
印　　　次：2017 年 6 月第 1 次印刷
书　　　号：ISBN 978-7-5641-7087-5
定　　　价：198.00 元

经　　　销：全国各地新华书店
发行热线：025-83790519　83791830

＊版权所有，侵权必究。
＊本社图书若有印装质量问题，请直接与营销部联系。电话：025-83791830